The Penti

A br.

John Young
2016

*'The time is come you plainly see,
The government opposed must be'*

Jeremiah Brandreth, 1817

Eebygumbooks
Bolsover
UK

www.eebygumbooks.co.uk

© *John Young, 2016*

No part of this book may be reproduced in any form or by any means, electronic, or mechanical, including photography, recording, or by any information storage or retrieval system or technologies now known or later developed without permission in writing from the publisher

Front cover from a print in Derby Local Studies and family History Library, used by permission.

Design and layout, John Young

Acknowledgements	4
Prologue	5
Jeremiah Brandreth	7
Hard Times, New Ideas	14
Paid Spies and Informers	18
Revolution	24
Flight and Capture	37
Oliver the Spy	42
The Trials	46
The Sentences of Those Found Guilty	56
Farewells	58
Retribution	62
Appendix 1: The Women	67
Appendix 2: Why There? Why Then?	70
Bibliography	76
Index	80

Acknowledgements

I first became fascinated by the Pentrich Revolution in about 1980 and this book has been a long time in its gestation. In the early 1980's Keith Jones and I wrote a series of songs and toured the Pentrich story around social clubs. Then Max Biddulph and I wrote the story as a student play at Spondon School, Derby which I later adapted for Central TV working with Director Norman Hull.

This short history includes modern research made available through the internet. Sylvia Mason's impressive genealogical research has opened up the family histories of most of the insurgents, notably Jeremiah Brandreth. Documents have been downloaded from the National Archives, The British Museum and elsewhere. I would especially like to thank the Derby Local Studies and Family History Library whose people are as enthusiastic and helpful today as they were all those years ago.

Sincere thanks to my lifetime friend, Paddy McEvoy who checked the manuscript and offered perceptive observations, not all in approval of the events portrayed. I am also most grateful to my son Paddy Young, for his close reading and discussion of the emerging text. Particular praise and thanks must go to the sharp-eyed and diligent Paul Iwanyckyj for scrupulous proof reading and correcting my error-strewn original drafts. To these and all who have informed this book over the years I offer my sincere gratitude and appreciation.

On June 9th, 1817, a few hundred ill-armed Derbyshire villagers marched out to demand the right to vote and a fairer society. They were duped, betrayed, fitted-up, slandered and savagely punished. Worst of all, their sacrifice was conveniently forgotten about, even by socialist historians. As their anniversary approaches, we have the chance to truly celebrate the sacrifices of the heroes and heroines of The Pentrich Revolution and this book is my contribution.

John Young, April, 2016

Prologue

Brandreth Beheaded from a contemporary print (Derby Local Studies and Family History Library, used by permission)

There was a public execution in Derby on Friday, November 7th, 1817. The *Derby Mercury's* correspondent observed the scene:

"The executioners put the caps upon the heads of the unhappy men and pulled them over their faces. Each of them exclaimed at this moment 'Into thy hands O God I commit my spirit.'...At twenty five minutes before one, the bolt was drawn and they were launched into eternity."

The bodies were then left hanging for half an hour before the first of the three dead men was cut down and his corpse laid upon a bench.

"The cap was then removed from the head and the neck having been pressed close upon the block, at twenty five minutes after one the executioner struck the blow. The head was not at once detached from the body; the blow appeared more feeble to the populace than it really was and a groan of horror was the consequence. The assistant, however, with one of the knives, instantly completed what had not been accomplished by the axe. The head fell in the basket, and the hangman, seizing it by the hair, held up the ghastly countenance of the Nottingham captain to the view of the multitude. He proceeded with it to the left, to the right and to the front of the scaffold, bearing the trunkless ball in his hand and exclaiming at each place 'Behold the head of the traitor, Jeremiah Brandreth" [1]

The other two bodies received the same abusive treatment and thus ended the lives of Jeremiah Brandreth, forty-six year old William Turner and fifty-two year old Isaac Ludlam. These were the last ever public beheadings in England.

The grisly deaths they suffered were punishment for the parts they played in the Derbyshire Rising of 1817, also known as 'The Pentrich Revolution'. This event is considered to be 'England's Last Revolution'.

---

[1] (Derby Mercury, November 9th, 1817)

Jeremiah Brandreth

At the time of his death, Jeremiah Brandreth, also known as John Coke and popularly called the 'Nottingham Captain', was a man of mystery. Awaiting execution, he avoided talking of his previous life and family. Rumour had it that he was from the Exeter area. He may have been a sailor or a tinker. He refused to shave for his trial and contemporary prints of Jeremiah show him as a bearded, piratical figure. Mr. Denman, his defending lawyer, described him as looking *'like the captain of an armed banditti.'*[2] According to one author *"he was a large, powerful man"*[3], but a spy who betrayed him said he was *"a little man, dark complexion, brown hair, wears whiskers."*[4] His execution was delayed while the noose was lowered to match his small stature, but many years afterwards one of his followers gave a different description: *'Tall, he was, and dark, with flashin' black eyes and a bog-black beard.'*[5]

The enigmatic Brandreth's place and date of birth have also been much debated. A contemporary account published in Derby, gave his birthplace as Exeter and his age as twenty-seven. Stevens[6] claims he was born in 1786 at Sutton-in-Ashfield and was thirty-one years old. The fact he moved to Wilton, near Nottingham, to claim relief may be significant, as under the Old Poor Laws claims were made in one's birth parish. Wilton's Parish Overseer testified at Brandreth's trial.

The recent biography[7] by John Dring which draws upon painstaking

---

[2] (Howell's State Trials: The Trial of Jeremiah Brandreth , 1824)

[3] (Black, 1969)p19

[4] (Stevens, 1977)

[5] (Parkin, 1817 A Recipe for Revolution, 2014)

[6] (Stevens, Op Cit)

[7] (Dring, 2015)

genealogical research by Sylvia Mason[8] has provided a much more informed history for Jeremiah Brandreth. This reveals that his father Timothy and his mother Mary married in London in 1780 and that Jeremiah, their fourth child, was born in Holborn, London, in 1785.

When Jeremiah was thirteen, the family moved to Barnstaple, Devon and five more children were born. Timothy worked with Mr March, a weaver from Leicester. In his conversations with Reverend George Pickering while in Derby Jail, Jeremiah mentioned he had been sent to school.[9] It can be supposed that this was The Bluecoat School, although pupil rolls do not exist; subsequently the family moved to Exeter. Flindell's Western Luminary asserts that Timothy was a stocking weaver living in Maudling Street and describes him as a radical sympathiser, someone who *'loved to cackle over his ale in the line of left-handed politics too.'*[10] In 1803 Jeremiah became an army reservist in the 28th North Gloucestershire Regiment of Foot stationed at Ottery St Mary in Devon.

John Dring suggests he was subsequently deployed to London as part of the guard at the execution of Colonel Despard and six guardsmen. He is then reported to have deserted and gone to Sutton-in-Ashfield where he had relatives.[11] Desertion might explain why Brandreth later chose to make no statement about his early life. Whatever his antecedents, he married a coalminer's daughter, Ann Bridgett of Bedlam Court, Sutton-in-Ashfield, in 1811 and by 1817 they had two children, Elizabeth aged four and Timothy aged two, with a third on the way. Though legally settled in the parish of Wilton and claiming Parish Relief, the Brandreths lived in Cross Court and also Butcher's Close, Nottingham.[12]

---

[8] (Mason)

[9] (Trial and Execution of the Traitors at Derby, 1817)

[10] (Bristol Mirror, 1817)

[11] (Dring, 2015)

[12] (Home Office, 1817)

Jeremiah, a skilled framework knitter, made top grade stockings in the Derby Rib pattern. The 'quality' end of the trade at which he made his living was subject to the vagaries of fashion in Regency England. Decorative stockings were an essential feature of male dress at a time when men wore breeches. Part of Brandreth's misfortune was to be working at a time when breeches and the cult of 'the elegant leg' were being replaced by pantaloons and trousers.

Hosiers who owned the expensive frames used by the knitters began to produce cheap 'shoddy' stockings that were made of reclaimed wool and stitched up the back. Little skill was needed and young people provided the cheap labour that was required. This practice was called 'colting'. Most hosiers paid at least a proportion of wages as credit through their own grocery stores which were often expensive and of low quality. This 'truck' system usually resulted in people becoming indebted to their employers. Home-based knitters who refused to buy from the truck shops often found the hosiers would reciprocate by rejecting their garments or increasing the rent on their frames.

Frustrated in their attempts to negotiate decent returns for their labour from the hosier merchants, the stockingers began to organise in response. The Combination Acts of 1799 and 1780 had made it illegal for groups of workers to establish societies or unions but they were also intended to prevent employers combining to fix prices. In 1811 Gravener Henson from Nottingham attempted to prosecute several hosiers under the Combination Acts. The hosiers wielded a lot of power locally (the Town Clerk was also clerk to the Hosiers' Committee) and the prosecution failed.

Henson subsequently set up the United Committee of Framework Knitters which many stockingers subscribed to. The committee hired lawyers to prepare a bill to be laid before Parliament to regulate the conduct of the hosiery trade and prevent the exploitation of the textile workers.

The *Bill for Preventing Frauds and Abuses in Frame-work Knitting*

Manufacture was funded by subscriptions from a wide range of people, including Lord Byron. Money was raised to pay lawyers and support Henson and others while in London. Heavily altered, the Bill passed its third reading in the House of Commons but was rejected in the House of Lords in July, 1812. The lobbying of the hosier merchants had proved to be too strong; radical leaders in Parliament wanted constitutional reform but would not become involved in trade disputes and offered no support to Henson.[13]

Alongside the peaceful process of petitions and attempting to change laws in Parliament, the first decade of the 19th century saw more direct action against the hosiers who were flooding the market with low-quality 'shoddy' goods and ruining the livings of the framework knitters.

There had been a tradition of smashing new machines such as the threshing machines and looms that put people out of work throughout the 18th Century. Much of this was localised and sometimes haphazard, but Luddism in Nottinghamshire was highly organised. Frame breakers in the midlands and northern counties claimed to be commanded by mythical General Ned Ludd from whom Luddism derived its name. In March, 1811, a demonstration by stockingers in Nottingham was dispersed by troops. Most of the crowd progressed to the village of Arnold where sixty frames were destroyed to the accompaniment of raucous celebration and cheers from the onlookers. Just a few months later, in November, frame breaking was no longer the work of sporadic 'rioters' but of small disciplined bands of masked Luddites, who moved rapidly from village to village after dark.[14] The Luddites were careful to only smash frames that were being used for "shoddy" work; others were left alone. The ferocity and efficiency of the Luddites frightened the hosiers and alarmed the government.

---

[13] (Thompson, 1968)p 587-590

[14] (Thompson Op Cit)

In Sutton-in-Ashfield, where the Brandreths were then residing, seventy frames were broken in one night and there is little doubt that Jeremiah was a committed Luddite. George Weightman, known to be an honest man, reported that Brandreth told him about his involvement in a Luddite attack at Basford.[15]

Frame breaking briefly ceased in the midlands from the beginning of 1812. This was because most hosiers were sufficiently intimidated to agree to buy at higher prices, additionally, the government brought in several thousand troopers and the Frame-Breaking Act of 1812 made it a hanging offence to smash frames. Although threats to the hosiers continued, no other major Luddite incidents occurred until 1814, when frame-breaking restarted. The hosiers and the authorities countered by offering huge rewards for information and the Home Office and local magistrates increasingly employed paid spies. In June, 1816, fifty-five frames were destroyed and a guard wounded at Heathcote and Boden's factory in Loughborough. Leading Nottingham Luddite, James Towle was recognised and hanged for his part in this episode in November, 1816; six more of his band were informed upon and suffered the same fate the next year.[16]

The secrecy and tight organisation of the Nottingham Luddites provided an excellent base from which to plan for a national rebellion in 1817. Interestingly, Brandreth's tactics during the rising of June 9th, 1817, bore a close resemblance to those often deployed by the Luddites.

Nottingham's population nearly tripled between 1750 and 1800, rising from 11,000 to 29,000.[17] This was almost entirely due to an influx of workers into the burgeoning textile industry. The city centre was soon turned into an area of slums that ranked amongst the worst in England.

---

[15] (Stevens, 1977) p103

[16] (Thompson, 1968) p626-627

[17] (Beckett)

There was a huge growth in worsted spinning, with Nottingham having 2,600 stocking frames in 1812. Although the population had burgeoned, building land did not expand significantly, and there was a rush to erect unplanned, poorly constructed back-to-back housing in a series of overcrowded courts with inadequate sanitation. Famous Nottingham streets like Broad Marsh and Narrow Marsh were well-named. The Brandreths lived in Butcher's Close and also Cross Court, off Cross Street, approximately where modern-day Huntingdon Street runs.

Before coming to Nottingham, Jeremiah and Ann Brandreth lived in Sutton-in-Ashfield where they married in 1811. Ann was born and bred in Sutton; Jeremiah seems to have had relatives in the area, but the precise connection is still unclear. In 1816, there were 1,700 unemployed persons claiming Parish Relief in Sutton and only 220 houses able to contribute to the poor rates. Consequently many people were removed to other parishes. The Brandreths were subject to a removal order to the parish of Wilton near Nottingham, on September 12th, 1816.[18] Hopeless poverty such as that suffered by Jeremiah and Ann gave rise to the discontent that made many in the midlands ripe for involvement in the tragic attempt to overthrow the government and which cost Jeremiah his life.

---

[18] (Dring, 2015)

A stockinger's house, Crich Common; large upper windows gave extra light. (Photograph, John Young)

Hard Times, New Ideas

In 1815 the Battle of Waterloo saw the final defeat of Napoleon and marked the end of years of protracted struggle in Europe. The aristocrats who governed Britain were shaken by the guillotining of the French aristocracy in 'La Grande Peur' (The Great Fear) in 1789, and the bloodshed of the French-backed Irish Rebellion of 1798. They were determined not to tolerate acts of domestic subversion that might lead to attempts to overthrow the regime by violence. The external threat may have passed, but in the years after Waterloo, Britain was convulsed by unrest rooted in the social dislocation caused by the rapid decline of a number of traditional industries. This destroyed home-based working and craftsmanship, replacing them with low wages, long hours and the exploitation of hundreds of thousands in the horrific conditions of the factories and textile mills.

In the century between 1750 and 1850 the philosophy of libertarian thinkers such as Tom Paine exerted great influence. Paine's writings inspired the generation of Americans who broke free from British rule in the War of Independence 1775-1783. Extracts from his works were read to Washington's troops at Valley Forge at a crucial point in the war; his *Rights of Man*, published in 1791-2 advocated a society based upon equality. He wrote in straightforward English accessible to ordinary people and had widespread influence in an England burdened with a dissolute Prince Regent and an unreformed Parliament dominated by landed interests and the old aristocracy.

Radical middle-class leaders like Cartwright, Cobbett, Burdett and Hunt urged reform of Parliament and relief for the poor but these urgent matters were not on the political agenda of the Conservative government of Prime Minister Lord Liverpool. The Home Secretary Lord Sidmouth dealt with unrest and social uproar in this period of chronic economic malaise in an increasingly confrontational style.

The slump following the Napoleonic Wars resulted in high unemployment further aggravated by the return of work-hungry soldiers and sailors. In March, 1817, Mr Brougham told the House of Commons that a third of the Yorkshire weavers were unemployed and only half the rest earned full wages.[19]

In Derbyshire, wrote Sir Henry Fitzherbert, *'a third of the population were thrown out of employment and became paupers.'*[20] Especially hard hit were framework knitters like Brandreth, whose high-quality hose was not in demand due to the vagaries of fashion and competition from cheap, 'shoddy' goods made of woolen waste and old rags run up on broad frames. With the final defeat of Napoleon in 1815, the purchase of stockings for the army diminished demand even further and even higher unemployment resulted.

Also in 1815 the Indonesian volcano, Mount Tambora, erupted. It was the largest such event in 1,300 years and the resulting dust cloud lowered temperatures across the globe. 1816 became Britain's 'year without a summer,' and the harvest was disastrous. In Buxton, Derbyshire, crops were not brought in until October.[21] Many parts of the country laid petitions before Parliament asking for relief of their distress but met with scant sympathy from a government that had just abolished income tax, paid by the rich, in favour of taxes upon necessities. Sir Francis Burdett's petitions to relieve distress were rejected in January 1817, and two others from Derbyshire presented by Lord G.H. Cavendish in February did no better.

In London serious trouble flared at two radical gatherings in the Spa Fields in Clerkenwell in late 1816, a year in which there was a growth in the number of Hampden Clubs across the country. Named after a radical from the English Civil War, the original club had been established by Major John Cartwright and others in 1812 as a society in which to debate how to reform Parliament and the government. These clubs were legal, but watched with suspicion by the government. In January, 1817, 70 delegates from Hampden Clubs

---

[19] (Brougham, 1817)

[20] (Fitzherbert, 1816)

[21] (Fitzherbert, ibid)

across Britain assembled at the Crown and Anchor in the Strand to agree a strategy for the reform of Parliament. A split emerged between those demanding annual parliaments, votes for all householders and fair constituency boundaries, and those who were less ambitious and perhaps more pragmatic. Another major disagreement was about using physical force to secure reform.

In the same month, the Prince Regent narrowly escaped injury when a missile was thrown through his carriage window as he returned from the opening of Parliament. This hardened the attitudes of the middle and upper classes against reform and they vented their outrage through loyal addresses criticising the reformers whose speeches incited unrest. Parliamentary Committees set up to investigate the Hampden Clubs, reported at the end of February that they were hotbeds of insurrection. They were numerous in Leicestershire and Derbyshire where their members were mainly distressed artisans who were considering turning to revolution if their aims were not soon achieved peacefully.

A major attempt to seek Government help to relieve distress took place in March, when weavers from the Manchester area attempted a peaceful march to London. They planned to carry a petition to ask for relief and take only a blanket each to protect them from the weather. Ten thousand Blanketeers assembled at St Peter's Church on March 11th, but troops quickly dispersed the meeting and only a few hundred were able to set off. Most turned back at Stockport following attacks by cavalry and scores were arrested.

A jittery government reacted by introducing four new laws:

- severe punishments were to be imposed for enticing soldiers and sailors from their allegiance to the throne;
- the Prince Regent's guard was strengthened
- powers to quell seditious meetings were increased
- The Habeas Corpus Act was repealed so suspected agitators could be held without trial.

Home Secretary Sidmouth asked the Lord Lieutenants of the counties for increased vigilance against those who were distributing 'blasphemous and seditious tracts'. By this he meant publications such as William Cobbett's *'Political Register'* and *'Twopenny Trash'* and Thomas Wooler's *'Black Dwarf'*. He also employed spies and informers to infiltrate the secret clubs and apprise him of their plans.

The English middle-class radical leaders

Major J Cartwright, 1740 - 1824[22]   Henry Hunt 1773 - 1835[23]

Sir Francis Burdett, 1770-1844[24]   William Cobbett, 1763-1835[25]

---

[22] (Unknown, n.d.)

[23] (Buck)

[24] (Maurin)

[25] (Unknown) Creative Commons

Paid Spies and Informers

One such informer, William Oliver, who became known as 'Oliver the Spy', played a major part in the events of June, 1817. A month after the rising Hiley Addington, Lord Sidmouth's brother, gave the House of Commons the official view of how Oliver came to be employed:

'Mr Oliver ... came to the Home Office at the beginning of April, 1817 and offered information which he considered beneficial to the country, but which he had not obtained by being implicated in any conspiracy. He asked no reward and never received a shilling from the Government, except that which served to defray his travelling expenses.'[26]

In light of Oliver's later record, and the fact that in 1816 he had spent some months in the Fleet Prison as a debtor, this last statement appears somewhat fanciful. Oliver's origins are as obscure as Brandreth's. What is known is that he adopted at least four aliases: he was known to some of the Nottingham radicals as Hollis, took the name Maule while waiting to be called as a witness in Derby in the autumn of 1817, signed his letters to Sidmouth as W J Richards (probably his real name) and finally made his will out as Jones! Imprisoned for debt in 1816 due to his failure as a builder/surveyor he was helped out of the Fleet Prison by a friend, Charles Pendrill, a well-known radical. Pendrill introduced Oliver to his circle of political acquaintances, including Joseph Mitchell, a Lancastrian of similar radical views, who was travelling the country speaking at Hampden Clubs and selling newspapers. He could not have a better set of introductions to the key radicals across the country.

According to Pendrill, Oliver:

'began to make very vehement professions of patriotism, and expressed uncommon anxiety to know whether there were any political

---

[26] (The Parliamentary Debates from the Year 1803 to the Present Time, Volume 36)

associations into which he might obtain admittance'[27]

Oliver also wrote to Sidmouth in April 1817 and entered his service as a secret agent. Mitchell and he began a tour of the Hampden Clubs of the midlands and north, leaving London on April 23rd. The pair visited Birmingham and then set off for Yorkshire. They changed coaches at the *Talbot Inn* at Derby and met with the landlord Robertshaw, a radical sympathiser. During this period Mitchell who was well-known to Hampden Club members throughout the country introduced Oliver to many key potential revolutionaries.

The spy signing in the name Oliver[28]

---

[27] (Cobbett, 1818)

[28] (Home Office, 1817)

As he journeyed Oliver sent his employer letters containing the names of those he met and their doings. His reports show him as an astute observer and a man capable of thinking on his feet. When Mitchell's proximity began to make this task difficult and dangerous, Oliver arranged with the Home Office to have him arrested in Huddersfield on May 4th. *'The Derby Mercury'* reported:

'The public will feel satisfaction in being informed, that Mitchell, one of the most celebrated, by his party, of the late junta of Political orators and reformers in this town is in custody.'[29]

The removal of Mitchell and the departure of Pendrill for America placed Oliver in the position of being able to invent information and news from London without anyone being there to contradict him, an advantage that he used to the full.

On May 5th, Oliver attended an important meeting in Wakefield, at *The Joiners Arms*, an inn owned by the radical Benjamin Scholes. By now known as the London Delegate, he met sixty-four year old Thomas Bacon the influential delegate for Derbyshire, Nottinghamshire and Leicester. They were secretly assembled to fix a date for a national rising to overthrow the government. Bacon, in a later statement claimed Oliver said that Cartwright and Burdett knew and approved of the meeting and took a leading part saying:

'something more must be done as Parliament refuses to institute an Enquiry into the distress of the people. London feels very much for the distress of the Country and is ready to turn out but they cannot remove it of themselves without the assistance of the Country at the same time."[30]

Oliver said that London would raise about seventy thousand in three hours and told the gathering the regions must turn out at the same

---

[29] (Derby Mercury, May 6th, 1817)

[30] (Bacon, 1817)

time to demand universal suffrage and annual parliaments.

If there is substance in Bacon's statement it is clear that Oliver was no mere informer, but someone attempting to provoke an uprising. He may have adopted this voluble style to endear himself to the other attendees, (he could hardly have remained silent!) but one cannot be sure whether he was acting on his own agenda or following the orders of the Home Secretary. Oliver next returned to London to report to Sidmouth, but soon he was heading up country again, protected by letters of introduction sent to the northern magistrates and Northern District Commander, Major General Sir John Byng.

He revisited Birmingham, called in again on Robertshaw at Derby and toured villages around Nottingham. He was in Sheffield on May 29th, then headed to Nottingham for a meeting at The Three Salmons where he possibly met Jeremiah Brandreth. He continued to claim that scores of thousands were poised to act in London and stressed how vital it was that the regions turn out in support.

Oliver was asked by William Wolstenholme leader of the Sheffield radicals (father of Hugh Wolstenholme the curate of Pentrich) to stay a second day for an evening meeting. He refused as he was already booked on the Leeds stage. This was a stroke of fortune for Oliver, because the local magistrate, Hugh Parker, acting on information from his own spy, had the building where about thirty Yorkshire radicals were meeting surrounded. The operation was botched however, and only Wolstenholme and three others were captured; the rest went into hiding. This was a near miss for Oliver and Sidmouth wrote to Parker urgently to ensure his spy would not be taken:

'It is however become necessary to inform you that O is employ'd by me; that he is travelling under my Directions at this Time.... I accordingly shall be anxious till I hear again & should be much relieved by hearing he has not been apprehended.'[31]

---

[31] (Stevens, 1977) p44

Oliver visited other towns in Yorkshire before crossing the Pennines to take in Liverpool and Manchester. On June 4th he met Major General Byng at Camps Mount and hatched a plan to capture delegates from Wakefield and elsewhere at a remote inn near Thornhill-Lees on June 5th. This was the planned final meeting to discuss last minute strategy for June 9th, the date agreed for the national rising. Byng took personal command of the operation to arrest the assembled leaders. Oliver was taken with the rest but it had been pre-arranged with Byng for him to escape.

He then travelled south from Wakefield to attend the final planning meeting of the Nottingham Committee at *The Punch Bowl Inn* on June 7th. News of the Yorkshire arrests had come in. Nottingham Committee Chairman William Stevens had actually set off to Yorkshire to attend the meeting at Thornhill-Lees but had been called back. Oliver's escape aroused suspicion, as did his smart clothes and his penchant for staying at expensive inns. Frightened he had been discovered, only pressure from local magistrates overcame his reluctance to attend the meeting at *The Punch Bowl*.

In a tense encounter Oliver underwent an aggressive interrogation from John Holmes and others who believed him to be a spy. He denied this vigorously and insisted it was vital he return to the London leadership to confirm the commitment of the north and midlands to support the rising. Holmes assured him that they were *"not so fond of being hung"* in Nottingham as they were in Yorkshire and for a time it must have seemed to Oliver that he was discovered. He kept his nerve however and eventually Committee Chairman William Stevens decided Oliver should leave the meeting before tactics for June 9th were discussed and allowed him to return to his expensive inn, *The Blackamoor's Head*.[32] The next morning Oliver fled to London having broken the Yorkshire leadership, sowed seeds of doubt in the minds of the Nottingham Committee, and sealed the fate of Brandreth and the Derbyshire rebels.

---

[32] (Cobbett's Political Register May 16th, 1818) p558

The Committee was clearly uneasy about Oliver, but seems to have decided to press on with the rising. No message of caution was sent to Pentrich, indeed Brandreth's emissary, Joseph Weightman, was assured by Stevens that all was well at a meeting at *The Plough* on Coalpit Lane, Nottingham on June 8th. (p 26) This was to prove the undoing of the Derbyshire men.

Henry Addington, Lord Sidmouth[33]

---

[33] (Copley)Public domain

Revolution

After meeting Oliver at Wakefield on May 5th, Thomas Bacon had returned home to Pentrich. Bacon wore his white hair long and when he preached he resembled an Old Testament prophet. He was instrumental in founding the Pentrich Hampden Club, and since 1791 had been *'an active supporter of the doctrines of Liberty and Equality and a zealous disciple of Thomas Paine'*. The authorities knew of 'Old Tommy' as an agitator and suspected him of being involved in Luddite machine-breaking activities in the Pentrich area. Retired from his trade as a framework knitter, Tommy travelled extensively as a radical delegate and was one of the participants at the Crown and Anchor rally in January, 1817. His later statements and writing abilities demonstrate a vocabulary far wider than one would expect of a man of his background and circumstances. Bacon was regarded by many as the architect of the Pentrich Revolution. He had been sacked from the local Butterley Ironworks for trying to politicize its large workforce and Goodwin the Manager later wrote:

'*Thomas Bacon is the great ringleader.*'[34]

On May 17th, Bacon called local sympathisers to a meeting at a Pentrich barn and revealed the date of the proposed rising as June 9th. This was the first of a series of meetings to make preparations for the rising. At a meeting at the *White Horse Inn* in Pentrich on June 5th, Bacon introduced a man sent from Nottingham to lead the Derbyshire villagers on June 9th. He was soon dubbed 'The Nottingham Captain' and named Jeremiah Brandreth.

Why this little unemployed framework knitter from the next county was chosen to lead a group of strangers in a place he did not know is uncertain. Thomas Bacon was clearly the principal figure in the area and the obvious choice to lead, but he claimed there was a warrant

---

[34] (Home Office, 1817)

out for his arrest and he needed to lie low. In any event, Bacon took no part in the march on June 9th and he later escaped hanging in consequence. Perhaps at the age of sixty-four and dependent upon his walking stick he feared he would slow down the march. After the rising, the *'London Packet'* explained:

'To secure impartiality on the part of the Generals, it was resolved that no person should have a command in the place to which he belonged. Generals were to be sent from Nottingham to Derby, from Derby to York and vice-versa.'[35]

Such a potentially disastrous tactic is highly questionable. Perhaps it was a device thought up by Oliver to further destabilize the rising? Whether this appraisal of the rebels' tactics is true or not, Brandreth quickly stamped his authority on the men who were to follow him. Witnesses later described how he exuded optimism about the rising and inspired his listeners.

At *The White Horse Inn,* on June 8th, Brandreth used a map to explain the route they would take and how they would conduct themselves. He had also written verses to be sung as they marched:

'Every man his skill must try,
He must turn out and not deny;
No bloody soldier must he dread,
He must turn out and fight for bread;
The time has come you plainly see,
The Government opposed must be'

The White Horse's landlady, Ann 'Nanny' Weightman, was sister to Thomas and John Bacon and mother to George and his three brothers, all of whom marched on June 9th.

She threatened to put Special Constables Anthony Martin and Shirley Ashbury up the chimney as she thought them spies. Both

---

[35] (London Packet and Lloyds Evening News, November 3rd, 1817)

testified at the subsequent trials.[36]

St Matthew's Pentrich across the road from where the White Horse Inn stood and where fugitives later hid. (photograph John Young)

During the eight hour meeting plans were discussed on how to capture Butterley Ironworks which was located between Pentrich and nearby Ripley. Some wanted the works to be commandeered and used to make cannon and shot. Brandreth disagreed, telling them that orders were to reach Nottingham without delay. To resolve the issue it was agreed to consult William Stevens and the Nottingham Committee. Joseph Weightman, Nanny's brother in law was sent off to get clarification and confirmation that all was set for June 9th. (Joseph attended a meeting at *The Plough Inn*, Nottingham where William Stevens assured him his men were determined to rise. He returned the next day, June 9th, and passed on the message.)

At the White Horse William Turner, a stone mason, and quarryman

---

[36] (TheTrials of Jeremiah Brandreth, William Turner, Isaac Ludlam, George Weightman and others, 1817) p95

Isaac Ludlam reported that the weapons at their disposal were mainly old spears, pikes and farm implements; there were very few firearms. Turner had travelled to radical meetings in other parts of the country and Ludlam and he were the leaders of the enthusiastic group living around South Wingfield and Wingfield Park. Elderly Isaac Ludlam was very religious and a Methodist lay-preacher. He had fathered fourteen children of whom only seven remained alive in 1817. William Turner, an old soldier who had served in Egypt, shared the house he had built with his parents. Both men were well-regarded in their community, although Turner occasionally lost his self-restraint when drunk. He was keen to settle with the local magistrate Wingfield Halton who had recently evicted local families in winter. Four local men were under sentence to be hanged for retaliating. Turner had a plan to 'draw the badger', which involved lighting a fire at Halton's door and shooting him when he came out.[37]

Obtaining more firearms and ammunition were obvious priorities for Brandreth who explained that they would use a Luddite tactic of waking up local residents, forcing anyone who owned a gun to hand it over and make all able-bodied men join the march.

Brandreth sent his 'army' home, stirred by the prospect of action and fired by promises of money, bread, beef and ale when they reached Nottingham. There they would link up with thousands from Yorkshire – the 'Northern Clouds' he called them. They would take boats on the Trent and capture Newark before proceeding to London. The government would fall and be replaced by one made up of the leading reformers, including Cartwright and Burdett.

On the night of June 9th, unaware that Lord Sidmouth and the local magistrates were well informed of their plans, Brandreth and the South Wingfield men assembled at a place known as Hunt's Barn. The date and details of the rising were known to the authorities through Oliver and other spies. Brandreth's specific role had been betrayed by Henry Sampson from Bulwell. Sampson was a friend of

---

[37] Stevens (1977)

Jeremiah's, but had been informing on the Nottingham leaders to Enfield the Town Clerk, for some time. He visited Brandreth's house on June 5th to find Jeremiah had just departed for Pentrich and that Ann his wife did not expect him to return until 'the job was done.'[38]

Present and prominent at Hunt's Barn was George Weightman, the likeable and enthusiastic son of Nanny Weightman and nephew to Thomas Bacon. George, who had two children with his wife, Rebecca, was to play an interesting part during the night ahead. Brandreth had earlier revealed his plans for recruiting more men and gathering extra weapons by rousing the neighbourhood and forcing householders to join the train, tactics familiar to former Luddites in his ranks. Accordingly, the Wingfield rebels began hammering on doors, demanding guns and pressing able-bodied men to join them.

Brandreth set the tone for the night at the second house they came to by levelling a gun at the reluctant head of the householder, Henry Tomlinson and threatening him with the severest consequences if he refused to join the rebellion. Like others that night, Tomlinson wisely capitulated and fell into line. George Weightman felt sorry for him and a little later helped him to escape back home to his wife.[39]

John Neal, in his book, 'The Pentrich Revolution', written closer to that time than today, describes the position of the Derbyshire farmers thus:

'in this manner honest English farmers were compelled to give up the guns which they had for the purpose of using in their own defence and which were afterwards converted into instruments for the destruction of their fellow subjects and the Government and Constitution of their country.' [40]

---

[38] (Home Office Papers 42/166, 1817)

[39] (Howell's State Trials: The Trial of William Turner p1004, 1824)

[40] (Neal, 1895)

Not all were reluctant to join Brandreth; farmer Samuel Hunt provided bread, cheese and beer for his visitors and joined the column with his servant, enthusiastically participating in later events.

The one fatality of June 9th occurred at the next farm, which belonged to a widow named Mary Hepworth and stood in Wingfield Park.[41] The slumbering household was aroused at midnight by the armed insurrectionists. Samuel Hunt, Mrs Hepworth's near neighbour, threw a large stone at her door. Despite this, the band failed to gain entrance to the stout farmhouse. Brandreth went to the rear of the building and forced open the shutters of the kitchen window. A pistol was discharged and mortally wounded Robert Walters a servant of the house who ironically had been lacing his boots in order to join the rising. Brandreth was blamed for shooting, but was never tried for this murder and later denied that he had fired the shot.

Meanwhile, the Pentrich section of rebels had been given the task rousing men and finding weapons in their area. Heavy rain was falling which put them off and they stayed dry sheltering in Asherfields Barn. When Brandreth's band arrived he was annoyed to find little had been achieved, and two hours were wasted as they set off to visit houses in the vicinity of Pentrich and press more reluctant conscripts into the ranks.

Old soldiers William Turner and Brandreth began to form the group into a column. Turner's nephew, Joseph 'Manchester' Turner, was appointed a lieutenant. This Turner, (nicknamed after the city he had recently returned from) had one good eye and had been a Blanketeer. Isaac Ludlam commanded the rear- guard. More houses were visited, and more reluctant volunteers added to the ranks. Many of these would re-surface at the subsequent trials as enthusiastic prosecution witnesses.

---

[41] (Howell's State Trials: The Trial of Jeremiah Brandreth , 1824) (pp408-9)

As the band regrouped at Pentrich, George Weightman was dispatched on a pony to fetch news of events in Nottingham.[42] The marchers turned down the hill towards the Butterley Ironworks. Founded in 1790, the works was the main employer in the area. Despite attempts by Bacon to convert them, the majority of the Butterley workers were not in favour of the rising. They had secure jobs and wished to keep them.

The owner of the works, William Jessop and Goodwin and Wragg his two managers knew there was to be a rising and had previously sworn in a hundred special constables in Ripley Market to defend the town and the ironworks; many of these were Butterley workers. By 3am on the morning of June 10th as no rebels had appeared most of the constables had been dismissed. Jessop, Goodwin and Wragg were still at the works with a few employees when the action began. Goodwin wrote later to Josiah Jessop, brother of William:

'It was now three o'clock in the morning of Tuesday the 10th, and we had just deposited the Pikes and the men were separating to go home, when a horseman, Geo. Weightman of Pentrich (son of the woman who keeps the 'White Horse') rode by. I called to him to stop - but he pushed forward – Another person was then seen on the road from Pentrich near the New Shop. Mr Jessop and Mr Wragg ran to see who it was. It was found to be Jno. Cope, and immediately afterwards the main body of the insurgents in number about one hundred appeared marching past Woodhouse's Garden in regular order.

'Rather more than half were armed with Guns the remainder with spears stuck in Shafts about twelve or fourteen feet long. Scythes fixed in Shafts. One or two with Forks and a very few without arms. As we had no guns and did not think it prudent to begin the attack, we ordered the men to retire into the Office, where we determined to defend ourselves with the Pikes.

---

[42] (Howell's State Trials: The Trial of Jeremiah Brandreth, 1824)

'The insurgents came forward in good order in a line formed two deep opposite the office extending in a curve from the front of the Garden Wall to the Doors of the Foundry Yard which were shut. The fellow at the head who acted as chief gave the words 'halt to the right face – front.

'He was a thin little man apparently not thirty years of age and was dressed in a long brown coat and armed with a Gun and pistols he knocked with the butt end of his Gun against the yard doors, I went to the office doors and asked, 'What do you want?' What is your object here?' He answered. 'We want your men.'

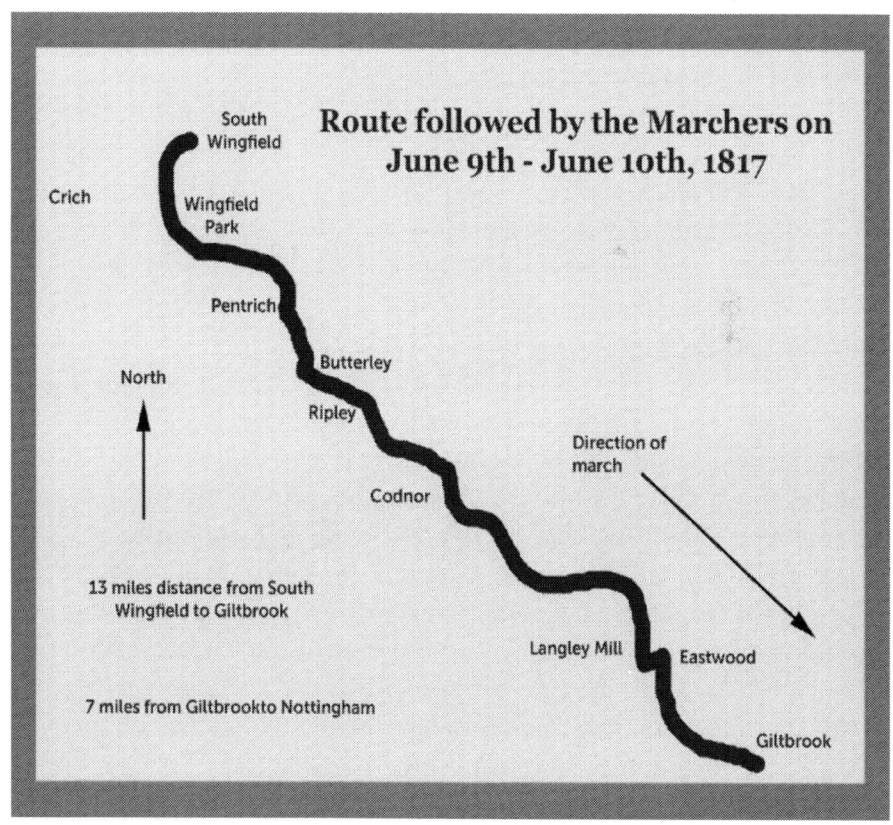

(Photograph John Young)

'I replied - 'You shall not have them; you are too many except your purpose was better - disperse - the Law will prove too strong for you - You will all be hanged!' No answer whatever was made to me and seeing Isaac Ludlam of Wingfield Park (who was armed with a spear) - his nephew Jas Taylor (with a Gun) and Isaac Moore of Pentrich Lane End a mason who worked for us formerly (who carried a fork), all of whom I knew well- I went out amongst them and expostulated with them and pushing them around by the shoulder bid them get home or they would all be hanged. Ludlam (who is a sort of Methodist parson) appeared more agitated and trembled violently when he said, 'I am as Bad as I can be - I must go on - I cannot go back.

'During the time I was speaking to these men three young fellows who had been compelled to follow slipped in behind me and got into the office under our protection and whether the chief thought us too strong to be attacked or whether he feared further defection amongst his men I know not but without saying a word or taking notice of what had been passing he gave the word 'March' and led his men past Woodhouse's house and over the Coke Hearth whence they crossed the Derby road at the top of the Brick Row and went forward to Ripley.'[43]

Much was made later of George Goodwin's courage in confronting so many armed men and this was doubtless a factor in the rebels leaving the works unmolested. Brandreth's priority however, was to get his men to Nottingham, as he was already late and did not need a protracted struggle this early in the rising. To his men, however, it must have seemed that he had backed down before Goodwin and would not have improved their confidence in him or his leadership. Subsequently, the marchers avoided the centre of Ripley as they believed constables were defending the town, and continued through Greenwich to Codnor. They continued to press men into service as they travelled. The court report of the evidence of George Jepson, a Butterley worker living in the village of Greenwich, explained why he

---

[43] (Home Office Papers 42/167, 1817)

reluctantly joined Brandreth:

'about half past three o'clock of the 10th of June last he was awoken by a number of Armed Men.... he was compelled to get up when four men entered his house with guns who insisted on his going with them. They told him they had shot one man and he would be shot if he refused to go when the Captain came up. They offered him a gun which he refused. He proceeded with the Mob to Codnor, where a man offered him a Fork and swore if he did not carry it he would be run thro.'[44]

It was raining heavily by now and Brandreth divided his wet, dispirited force to briefly rest at three inns: *The Glass House, The French Horn* and *The New Inn*. At *The Glass House*, he refused to pay the score on the grounds that the Bank of England money would soon be worthless! After Codnor the group plodded on towards Langley Mill; by now many of the pressed men were thoroughly dejected and the march slowed further.

At Langley Mill, George Weightman and his pony reappeared, back from the outskirts of Nottingham. Brandreth conversed quietly with him for a few moments and then Weightman announced that all was going well in the city, the castle was taken, the soldiers would not stir out of their barracks and the Derbyshire men must come on. George had been given news by a man waiting for him on the outskirts of the city. This was probably William Stevens the Nottingham leader. His men had certainly mustered on Racecourse earlier, but in much fewer numbers than expected. Without Brandreth's delayed band they had dispersed, doing no more than threaten residents Mr Roper and Mr Percival, before returning to their homes.[45] Brandreth may have suggested that George exaggerate Steven's message which probably did not mention the castle being taken or the soldiers remaining in their barracks.[46]

---

[44] (Howell's State Trials: The Trial of Jeremiah Brandreth , 1824)

[45] (Howell's State Trials: The Trial of Jeremiah Brandreth , 1824) (p 851)

[46] (Stevens 1977) p68-69

The ruins of Butterley Ironworks today; the hexagonal office where George Goodwin stood his ground is front, left. (John Young)

Encouraged by the welcome but false information that Nottingham was already taken by insurgents, Brandreth's diminishing band continued advancing towards Eastwood calling for more refreshment at *The Junction Navigation Inn* (today called *The Great Northern*) and *The Sun Inn* (later the birthplace of the Midland Railway Company). At Eastwood, folk were out of their houses and in a state of great agitation. Rumours spread that a magistrate had ridden to the barracks to bring soldiers to confront the rebels. News that the soldiers would be on their way soon caused even more restlessness in the crumbling ranks and a number tried to desert. Brandreth took a firm stand against Henry Hole who was trying to leave. He fired at him as he walked away, but fortunately for Henry, Brandreth's arm was struck by Thomas Turner and the shot missed. Hole walked free to become yet another hostile witness later on.[47]

---

[47] (Howell's State Trials: The Trial of Jeremiah Brandreth , 1824) (p842)

Troops were indeed on the way. Lancelot Rolleston a local magistrate had spotted Brandreth's marchers before they reached Eastwood and ridden to Nottingham Castle to rouse the 15th Light Dragoons, commanded by Captain Frederick Philips. In addition to the Captain, there was just one NCO and eighteen privates at the Castle Barracks. As they and Rolleston sallied forth, two other magistrates, Mr Munday and Mr Kirkby joined them.[48]

As the confrontation neared, the insurgents were reinforced by groups who had caught up with them. They now included recruits from Heage, Belper, Crich, Swanwick, South Wingfield, Pentrich, Butterley, Ripley and elsewhere. These replaced the increasing numbers of deserters. Perhaps two hundred wet and apprehensive men briefly faced the charge of the soldiers at the Giltbrook stream in the early morning of June 10th. The rebels broke and ran almost immediately, tossing away pikes and guns, taking to the fields and woods to avoid pursuit. Many were arrested during the succeeding hours, having been hunted down enthusiastically by the soldiers and the local yeomanry.

Miles Bacon, son of John and nephew of Thomas recalled the scene many years later:

"Then one of us saw the redcoats. 'Soldiers!' he shouted at th' top of his voice, and we saw them. There looked to be a lot of them, but I were told after there were only ten and a magistrate. My father and mi brother were at th' head and they shouted – 'Run Miles! Soldiers!' and I ran ..."

Miles returned to Pentrich and hid for some days in a local hay barn with, amongst others, George Weightman. Eventually soldiers arrived and Miles fled across the fields and jumped across the Cromford Canal. He reached Leicestershire where he found work at a farm and eventually married, naming his eldest son 'Jeremiah'. He returned years later once the coast was clear to bring his mother out

---

[48] (Howell's State Trials: The Trial of Jeremiah Brandreth , 1824)

of the workhouse and settle in Belper, eventually feeling secure enough to register on the national census.[49]

> The commanding officer of the 15th Hussars who dispersed the insurgency was Frederick Charles Philips who joined regiment in 1808 and became a captain in 1812. He rose to become a Lieutenant Colonel in 1826, before retiring in 1833. He had previously fought in the Corunna Campaign of 1808-9 and at Toulouse and been awarded the Peninsular medal. He also fought at Waterloo with the Fifteenth. He died in Italy in 1858. (Wylly, 1914)

> Lancelot Rolleston, the Nottingham magistrate who reconnoitered the rebels lived at Watnall Hall. His monument in the south aisle of the Church of Greasley St Mary reveals he was Colonel of The Sherwood Foresters Militia, Chairman of Quarter Sessions and Member of Parliament for Nottingham Southern Division from 1837 to 1849. He died in 1862, aged seventy six. (Southwell, 2016)

---

[49] (Parkin,1817 A Recipe for Revolution 2014)

Flight and Capture

Of the major leaders, William Turner was soon captured in a ditch near Langley Mill, together with his younger brother, Edward. With Turner incarcerated in Derby Jail, the hue and cry continued after Brandreth, Weightman, Ludlam and Bacon.

George Weightman was taken at Eccleston near Sheffield on July 16th, at the house of a relative of the curate of Pentrich, Hugh Wolstenholme, a radical member of a radical family. Wolstenholme had hidden George at his own house and also smuggled food to other escapees hiding in a local hayloft, narrowly avoiding arrest himself.[50]

The two constables involved in the taking of Weightman, Fletcher and Booth were in action the next week, when they arrested Isaac Ludlam at Uttoxeter on July 22nd. [51] On the same day, Brandreth was taken at Bulwell. After the rebels were dispersed at Giltbrook, the Nottingham Captain fled southwards and may have worked his way to Brighton, where his sister lived, and thence to Bristol. Here he tried unsuccessfully to board ships going to America. Penniless and friendless, he returned north and visited Sutton-in-Ashfield, where Ann had moved back in with her father. It was unsafe to stay so he contacted his 'friend' Henry Sampson, unaware that he was an informer. Sampson hid Brandreth in his house and then told the authorities about the arrival of his guest. Magistrates Rolleston and Mundy carefully planned the arrest, as Brandreth was suspected of being armed with a pistol and knife. (In fact, he had probably sold them.) Constable Benjamin Barnes and four others who came for him pretended they were looking for snares, as a device to protect Sampson's identity. Brandreth was 'recognised' and taken; the newspapers announced the welcome capture of the 'General of the

---

[50] (Home Office, 1817) (p42/170)

[51] (Stevens, 1977) p77

Insurgents.[52] He was taken to Derby Jail to join many of his comrades. As a relative stranger who had led his men to disaster, Jeremiah must have been concerned about his reception, but soon a spirit of comradeship was spreading throughout the jail.

Thomas Bacon and his brother John were taken on August 11th by Constable Henry Newton and others at St Ives in Huntingdonshire after a struggle. In the time they were in hiding, there had been 'sightings' of them all over England and rumours spread they were sailing for America. On good information constables were dispatched from Derby to Liverpool with a warrant, but the Bacon brothers were a long way from there. No doubt some of these reports were deliberately generated by Tommy Bacon's network of sympathisers, although a reward of one hundred guineas may have also been a factor. They were transported to Derby Jail, where Eaton, the jailer, was holding the other principals in the rising.

The same edition of the *'Derby Mercury'*, which announced the capture of the Bacons, described the execution of four men, one of them from Pentrich, hanged for firing the ricks of Colonel Wingfield Halton the South Wingfield magistrate. The *'Mercury'* concluded that these men would probably have joined the rising had they been at liberty. This view was echoed by William Lockett, the Derby Government Solicitor.[53] At the burial of one of the four at Pentrich, Hugh Wolstenholme preached a sympathetic radical sermon to the extreme disapproval of the authorities.

The Derby rebels were indicted at the Summer Assizes but their trials were put off until the year's excellent harvest was gathered. Given the awful harvest of 1816, local farmers would be very unwilling to serve as jurors with corn still in the field and an October date was set. While the prisoners lingered in the jails of Derby and Nottingham, the *'Derby Mercury'* was celebrating:

---

[52] (Home Office, 1817) (p42/168)

[53] (Home Office, 1817) (p42/168)

'Early this morning the bells of the different churches in this place announced the second anniversary of the ever memorable Battle of Waterloo, which has been celebrated with suitable rejoicings. At noon all the brave men at present in Derby who were engaged in the action decorated with their medals and well-merited laurels, were regaled with an excellent dinner at The New Inn and spent the afternoon with the utmost harmony and conviviality.'[54]

For old soldier, William Turner, who had fought Napoleon in Egypt, excellent dinners and conviviality were not the order of the day. During their early captivity, the prisoners (except the farmer Samuel Hunt who could afford better) lived upon bread and water because they had no means of purchasing a better diet. Eventually the danger that some of them might die of malnutrition before trial led Lockett the Derby solicitor to authorise the addition of small amounts of meat and vegetables, the costs of which he billed to The Home Office.

Once The Nottingham Captain had been captured fears for security in the overcrowded jail so concerned Lockett that he sought Home Office approval for Brandreth and the other principals in the rising to be put into full sets of irons though not yet charged.[55] He, Turner, Ludlam, Weightman and Bacon suffered great discomfort throughout their stay in Derby Jail. Sixty-four year old Thomas Bacon must have experienced particular inconvenience.

The jail had been built sixty years earlier in the part of the town known as Nun's Green. Both male and female prisoners were held here, and there were three small rooms for debtors, separate from the cells of the felons. The building was quite adequate to contain twenty prisoners in fairly humane conditions. Unfortunately, while the Pentrich rebels were incarcerated there, the total number was in excess of sixty, and the overcrowding meant that the men were sleeping in a seated position, six or seven to a cell at night.

---

[54] (Derby Mercury, 1817) (June 18th)

[55] (Home Office 1817) 42/168

Derby Jail today. 6,000 witnessed the executions here in 1817 (photograph John Young)

Each cell was ventilated at the top of its door by a grill which opened onto the passage outside it. The day room could not physically hold all those who were supposed to frequent it, and on all but the most inclement days, the inmates had to spend all their time in the prison yard. [56]

---

[56] (Stevens, England's Last Revolution 1977)

Brandreth in irons (Derby Local Studies and Family History Library, used by permission)

Oliver the Spy

During the period between June 9th and the commencement of the trials in Derby in October, there was much public indignation about the government's use of paid spies and informers. In particular, concern was expressed over the part Oliver had played. Accusations were made in Parliament and elsewhere that he had invented and provoked the rising on behalf of the Home Secretary.

Four days after the rising the *"Leeds Mercury'* journalist Edward Baines exposed William Oliver for the spy he was. The paper had information from John Dickenson of Dewsbury, a Yorkshire radical, who had escaped arrest in Sir John Byng's ambush at Thornhill-Lees and seen Oliver shortly afterwards in conversation with Byng's liveried servant.[57] Fair-minded people were offended that an *agent provocateur* might have been at the root of the Pentrich rising and induced men to rebel who would not have done so otherwise.

A furious Sir Francis Burdett asked in Parliament whether Sidmouth had given Oliver the authority to use his (Burdett's) name when inciting rebellion. It appeared that: *'Oliver ... had gone about the country introducing himself 'with Sir F. Burdett's compliments."* In reply, Lord Castlereagh denied that such authority had been given and defended Sidmouth's employment of Oliver and any other methods necessary to 'preserve the peace of the country'.[58]

The week after the rising Earl Fitzwilliam, Lord Lieutenant of Yorkshire wrote to Sidmouth that it was widely believed that the event due to *'the presence and active agitation of Mr Oliver'*.

Sidmouth replied that he found this *'incredible':*

---

[57] (Baines, Leeds Mercury, 1817)

[58] (Hansard, Vol36 cc1069-70, 1817)

'It is directly at variance with the instructions given to Oliver and with his communications to Sir John Byng (the Military commander in the North), as well as to myself... It would have been entirely inconsistent with the instructions given him by Government if he had in any instance fomented or encouraged the disaffected to proceed with greater activity or to greater lengths than they were themselves inclined to do.'[59]

Writing in 1820, Edward Baines, who was well-connected with radical leaders in Yorkshire, unequivocally condemned Oliver for inventing and promoting the idea of a national rising on June 9th:

'To ascribe to Oliver the entire production of all the sedition and treason which broke out during his operations would be absurd. He found the seeds of disaffection already scattered, and undoubtedly many had formed the opinion which he professed, that a redress of the nation's grievances was only to be obtained by force. But he found no plot. The materials at most, were existing, which he so assiduously gathered together, and worked up into a conspiracy; and the materials themselves he did his utmost to increase. The evil-disposed were few, obscure, remote from each other, without character, destitute of confidence as of strength: he augmented their numbers, brought them into connexion and concert, encouraged them by his personal appearance his pretended mission and his assurances, and presented to their ignorant and discontented minds the fair prospect of a complete revolution... no evidence has ever been given, to prove the existence of a treasonable confederacy before that formed by Oliver. To the acts of a government spy, then, may be ascribed the death of those men who were executed at Derby...'[60]

Baines was writing from the perspective of a radical journalist, but he had thoroughly investigated the movements of Oliver in May and

---

[59] (Aspinall, 1996)

[60] (Baines, 1820)

June, 1817, and spoken with many that heard the 'London Delegate'. He was also at pains to point out that he had taken care not to rely on an individual's statement unless there was evidence to support it. A number of the radical leaders independently said the same thing. William Stevens, safe in America, wrote how Oliver had used his final meeting in Nottingham to pressure the local men not to desert the Londoners in their revolt on June 9th.[61] In Derby Jail Brandreth and Turner blamed Oliver and the government for their troubles. Oliver's name was reviled across the country; one poor London butler mistaken for him was beaten up by a mob.[62]

Cruikshank's illustration from 1817. Sidmouth, Castlereagh and Canning with spies, including Oliver. John Bull laments: 'Poor starving John is to be ensnared into Criminal acts ...'[63]

---

[61] (Cobbett Op Cit p557)

[62] (Spies and Bloodites!!! No. 1(-3). 1817)

[63] (Cruikshank) Public Domain

The following table shows the extent of Oliver's energetic journeying from April to June. [64]

Oliver's Journeys, April to June, 1817

April 23	London	May 14	Sheffield
April 25	Birmingham	May 15/16	Back in London
April 26	Derby , Sheffield	May 24	Birmingham
April 27	Dewsbury	May 24-25	Derby
April 28	Wakefield	May 25, 27	Nottingham, local villages
April 29	Leeds	May 29	Sheffield, Wakefield
April 30	Middleton, Manchester	May 30	Bradford, Halifax
May 1- 3	Liverpool	May 31	Manchester
May 3 4	Manchester	June 1– 2	Liverpool
May 5	Wakefield	June 3	Leeds, Horbury
May 6	Huddersfield, Horbury, Ossett, Dewsbury	June 4	Camps Mount near Wakefield (Major General Byng)
May 7	Leeds	June 5	Leeds
May 8	Wakefield	June 6	Dewsbury, Thornhill, Wakefield
May 9	Barnsley	June 7	Nottingham
May 11 –12	Milnsbridge, Dewsbury	June 8	Birmingham
May 13	Leeds	June 11	Back in London

---

[64] (Baines, History of the Reign of King George III King of the United Kingdom of Great Britain and Ireland, 1820) p79

The Trials

On October 14th the Chief Baron of his Majesty's Court of Exchequer, Sir Richard Richards and the three other judges who were to conduct the trial, arrived at Derby. Ten lawyers for the prosecution, led by the Attorney General and the Solicitor General had been assembled. The prisoners had engaged the Manchester lawyer, John Cross, as their counsel. His demand for £100 in advance took most of what had been collected for the defence fund for which many of the defendants' families had sold their furniture. A disgusted Henry Hunt wrote later:

"Thus by the cupidity of Mr Cross, were these poor fellows deprived at once of those means which ought to have been spent in procuring them witnesses for their defence."[65]

Fortunately, Thomas Denman, an able lawyer from Nottingham who had defended Luddites at trials in 1815 was prepared to act without a fee. He was clearly up against a well-marshalled British establishment:

'The composition of the Grand Jury, double normal size, gave new meaning to the phrase `jury by peers'! For it was comprised of the cream of Derbyshire's ruling class: - nobility, rich farmers and textile tycoons crammed the jurors' seats.' **[66]**

After much deliberation, the prosecution decided to put Jeremiah Brandreth on trial first, and then proceed singly against William Turner, Isaac Ludlam and George Weightman. Thomas Bacon who had done so much to make Pentrich and South Wingfield such fertile ground for revolution was not to be tried with the other leaders. The sequencing of the trials is interesting, as the authorities had made it clear that they saw Bacon as the chief villain of the piece. To explain

---

[65] (Hunt, 1820-22) p504

[66] (Stevenson, 2004)

this one must look again to Oliver the Spy. Bacon was the only one of the defendants to have certainly met him; whilst incarcerated he had written a paper in which he recalled exactly what Oliver had said in the meetings he attended.[67]

Derby Courthouse today; the exterior has changed little since 1817 (Photograph John Young)

Other attendees wrote letters that the defence could have used to confirm the part that the spy had played in fomenting the discontent. Although brought to Derby under the name of 'Maule', Oliver was never called as a witness, to the government's obvious relief. Once the press had discovered he was in hiding in the city, it was thought expedient to send him south with all speed. *'The Leeds Mercury'* disclosures turned Oliver into an object of hatred. Elsewhere, yeoman juries returned verdicts of 'not guilty' in a number of cases where informers had been involved. The remnants of the Yorkshire

---

[67] (Bacon, 1817)

rebels, who had made a half- hearted attempt to rise at Huddersfield on June 9th, were never punished and their leaders were acquitted by juries disgusted at the employment of secret agents.

On Wednesday, October 15th, at 6am twelve prisoners held in Nottingham were escorted to Derby under armed guard. The city was packed and alive with rumour and interest. No less than three hundred jurors had been summoned and the prosecution had called two hundred and sixty eight witnesses. The Chief Baron opened proceedings by forbidding publication of the trials until they were finished and then a heavily bearded Jeremiah Brandreth was brought in with thirty five others to hear the indictment which claimed that they:

'together with a great multitude of false traitors, whose names are to the said jurors unknown, to the number of five hundred and more arrayed and armed in a warlike manner, that is to say with swords, pistols, clubs bludgeons and other weapons....did then with great force and violence, parade and march in a hostile manner, in and through divers villages, places and public highways... and did then and there maliciously and traitorously attempt and endeavour by force of arms, to subvert and destroy the Government and Constitution of this realm as by law assembled...'

To the long and complicated charge all thirty-five prisoners pleaded 'not guilty'.[68]

The prosecution needed to proceed in a very circumspect manner to keep Oliver from testifying at all costs. Sir Samuel Shepherd the Attorney General, who was an excellent lawyer, though deaf, came to an understanding with Denman and Cross. It was agreed that after the four deemed to be the main leaders had been tried, Bacon and the others would be spared the death sentence if they changed their pleas to 'guilty'. Brandreth and the other three had never met Oliver. Trying them first meant the spy would not be a material witness.

---

[68] (Howell's State Trials: The Trial of Jeremiah Brandreth , 1824)

At 10.30 a.m. October 15th, Jeremiah Brandreth was brought alone into court. Sir Samuel Shepherd rose to deliver a long address, outlining the events leading up to and including, June 9th and June 10th, dwelling on the death of Robert Walters and on Brandreth's role as 'Captain' of the rebels.

Many witnesses were called, notably: Special Constables Martin and Ashbury who had been at the meeting at *'The White Horse'* on June 8th; outraged farmers Mr. Tomlinson, Elijah Hall and Mary Hepworth; pressed man Henry Hole; Butterley works manager George Goodwin; Magistrate Lancelot Rolleston; and Captain Frederick Philips. Their evidence constituted an account of the rising that was entirely damning for Brandreth.

His counsel, Cross, in defence of Brandreth, blamed the government for failing to suppress Cobbett's *'Political Register'* and *'Twopenny Trash'*, which he described as the:

'most wicked and diabolical publications that were ever addressed to man'

Cross claimed it was such writings that had turned his client in the direction of revolution. The defence's aim was to prove that Brandreth had been seduced by the seditious words of better-educated radicals. It was also the aim to have the charge of High Treason, seen as inappropriate for such a small-scale attempt, replaced by a lesser. The deal between the defence lawyers and Shepherd meant one of the chief promoters of the rising, Oliver, was not called as a witness or even mentioned.[69]

Three years later, Denman explained there was no point in calling Oliver as Brandreth's treason was not to be mitigated in any way, even if the spy could have been shown to have incited it. He had killed a man and a succession of witnesses confirmed him to be the leader of the insurrection. Brandreth's cause in court was already

---

[69] (Howell's State Trials: The Trial of Jeremiah Brandreth, 1824)

lost, and the preservation of Oliver's anonymity became a lever to persuade the Prosecutors to be lenient towards the other prisoners.

On Saturday, October 18th, the jury retired to consider a verdict. After only twenty-three minutes they pronounced Brandreth guilty of High Treason. This was the first time ever a 'commoner' had been so charged and convicted. It had previously been levelled only at members of the nobility who had been involved in plotting directly against the life of the monarch. For most people in England, including many of the upper classes, the charge was seen to be preposterous. The court adjourned. At the announcement of the judgment Brandreth cast his eyes around him and retired in silence.

There was a long report in the 'Derby Mercury' lamenting that despite the instructions of the Chief Baron, some of the London journalists had the temerity to publish the first part of the trials. Extracts from these reports throw a great deal of light upon the personality of Brandreth as he endured the court proceedings:

'A more than usual paleness invaded his cheek, a faint perspiration was observed to overspread it and all the horrors of his situation appeared to burst on his imagination'

He was treated with great humanity and tenderness by those about him:

'As they knew him to be much in the habit of smoking, he was asked if he would like a pipe. He replied in the affirmative and a small part of a tobacco pipe, not more than three inches in length was brought to him... he received it with an awkward bow of gratitude, placed it in his mouth and immediately began to smoke in court.'

He accepted a glass of 'Negus' (port, lemon, hot water, sugar and nutmeg) and refused to make any statement for the newspapers. A long paper of sandwiches was given to him:

'He endeavoured to put them in his hat but the liberality which supplied him could not be compressed within such narrow limits

And he was advised to carry them in his hand.

'Upon this he wrapped them in an old blue handkerchief. The word 'ready' was now given from without to announce the caravan to be waiting for him. He hastily drank up what remained of his Negus and carrying his sandwiches with him was conveyed out of the hall by the back door.'

When Brandreth returned to the prison his fellows flocked around asking for news. He uttered the word 'guilty'. The others fell silent. [70]

William Turner's trial began on Monday, October 20th, 1817. The defence strategy was to demonstrate that Turner and the rest were led into the insurrection by the promises and personal magnetism of Jeremiah Brandreth. Similar prosecution witnesses were called to those in Brandreth's trial. Cross tried to show the naivety of the rising and argued that their deluded actions were not High Treason:

'The infantry, the formidable body of infantry, were armed with a dozen fowling pieces and two score of pikes. Well, and what was their cavalry? They had provided themselves with a pony and this was all the cavalry they had As to their ammunition, a single parcel of bullets was all that had been exhibited...one man, a pauper from Nottingham, had been styled 'generalissimo.' [71]

Turner was found guilty of high treason, as was Isaac Ludlam, whose trial began on Wednesday, October 22nd, during which Cross described Brandreth's arrival in Pentrich:

'a man of extraordinary character and a stranger, who placed himself with a map in a public house in the middle of the day and spoke in most imposing language to the villagers who were collected to hear him.'

---

[70] (Neal, 1895)

[71] (Howell's State Trials: The Trial of William Turner p1004, 1824)

Thomas Denman, 1779 - 1854[72]

Denman finally introduced Oliver's role in provoking the rising, though he did not mention him by name. He just talked of *'the principal author of the disturbances.'*

Of Brandreth he said:

'The captain was indeed a most extraordinary character. There was a wild daring in his look, a desperate decision in his manner and a furious energy in his conduct which bespoke the man capable of a commanding influence upon minds.'

---

[72] (Hodgetts)

Denman went on to compare Brandreth to Byron's 'Corsair'.[73]

George Weightman came to trial next. He appeared as *'a fine-looking young man who, notwithstanding his confinement, had a very high colour and a blooming countenance.'*

He was found guilty but one of the jurors, John Endsor of Parwich, was difficult to persuade. As verdicts had to be unanimous, George was unlucky not to walk free. This showed how disgusted even a loyal farmer could be about the role of government spies in the rising. It was recorded that:

'the Jury found the prisoner Guilty; that he had no lands &c. to their knowledge; and that they strongly recommended him to Mercy, in consideration of his former character.'[74]

On the tenth day of the trials, nine prisoners, including the Bacons, Samuel Hunt and 'Manchester' Turner were placed at the bar of the court. Denman announced that they wished to change their plea to 'guilty'. Another ten were brought in and they made a similar plea. The prosecution had no objection. Although they faced the death sentence for High Treason, the prosecution had promised to ask for mercy. They subsequently received sentences of transportation or imprisonment.

The twelve prisoners remaining, including three Weightmans, two Ludlams and a Turner walked free, the prosecution offering no evidence against them. The Chief Baron gave them a lecture:

'Thank God that you are spared. Endeavour to live sober and religious lives, and strive day and night to reform yourselves, so that you may become a credit to society, so that your days may be passed in some comfort here and be followed by a happy eternity.

---

[73] (Howell's State Trials: The Trial of Isaac Ludlam, 1824)

[74] (TheTrials of Jeremiah Brandreth, William Turner, Isaac Ludlam, George Weightman and others, 1817) p490

Go home, thank God and, SIN no more!'

After some moments of bewilderment, the freed men left the court and emerged into a crowd that was cheering the news. They were escorted by happy sympathisers and treated to food and drink amidst great celebration of their release.

Then the nineteen who had pleaded guilty including Thomas and John Bacon, Joseph 'Manchester' Turner and Samuel Hunt were brought into court for sentencing, followed by Brandreth, Turner, Ludlam and Weightman. When asked if he had anything to say, Brandreth replied:

'Let me address you in the words of our Saviour; if it be possible, let this chalice pass from me, but not my will, but your Lordships' be done.'

Turner and Ludlam asked for mercy, but George Weightman was silent. In pronouncing sentence, the Chief Baron became very emotional and had to cut short his address. He ended by condemning Brandreth, Turner, Ludlam and Weightman and the rest to death:

'.. each of you to be taken hence to the jail whence you came, from whence you must be drawn on a hurdle to the place of execution, and there to be severally hanged by the neck until you are dead; your heads must then be severed from your bodies, which are to be divided into four quarters and to be at his Majesty's disposal'

Ludlam reacted emotionally but Brandreth and the other two remained calm. The four were led away.

The two Bacons, Samuel Hunt, 'Manchester' Turner and six others had their sentences commuted to transportation for life to Australia. Three others were to be transported for fourteen years. Six more received short jail sentences.

The reformer, Henry Hunt, who watched Brandreth's trial from the front row, was most unhappy with what transpired:

"The means taken to procure tractable juries were the most barefaced and abominable; and jurors were mostly selected from amongst the tenantry of the Duke of Devonshire, the prisoners had not the slightest chance of escape, even if Mr Cross had done his duty; but, so far was he from doing it, that he actually confessed the guilt of his clients, and urged as a palliation that they were led into insurrection by reading the writings of Cobbett ... and although Mr Denman made an eloquent appeal to the jury, yet he could not remove the impression which had been left upon the minds of the jurors by the precious pleadings of Mr Cross."[75]

Hunt had tried with little success to raise funds in London to support the defence of Brandreth and the others. Burdett, Cartwright and the rest were trying to distance themselves from the rising, fearing it had damaged the cause of reform.

Although the trials were a national story, well-covered in the press, the non-appearance of Oliver was a great disappointment to the journalists who had flushed him out of his hiding place at The George Inn and hounded him back to the safety of London. The Nottingham Review described it as being like the eclipse of the sun, with one part illuminated (that of Brandreth and the Derbyshire rebels) and the other (Oliver's role) being in darkness.[76]

---

[75] (Hunt, 1820-22)

[76] (Stevens, England's Last Revolution 1967) p84

The Sentences of Those Found Guilty

EXECUTED
Jeremiah Brandreth, 31, Sutton in Ashfield, framework knitter
Isaac Ludlam, 52, South Wingfield, quarry worker
William Turner, 46, South Wingfield, mason
TRANSPORTED FOR LIFE
Thomas Bacon, 64, Pentrich, framework knitter
John Bacon, 54, Pentrich, framework knitter
George Brassington, 33, Pentrich, miner
German Buxton, 31, Alfreton, miner
John Hill, 29, South Wingfield, framework knitter
Samuel Hunt, 24, South Wingfield, farmer
John Mackesswick, 38, Heanor, framework knitter
John Onion, 49, Pentrich, iron worker,
Edward Turner, 34, South Wingfield, mason
Joseph 'Manchester' Turner, 18, South Wingfield clerk
George Weightman, 26, Pentrich, sawyer
TRANSPORTED FOR FOURTEEN YEARS
Thomas Bettison, 35, Alfreton, miner
Josiah Godber, 54, Pentrich, labourer
Joseph Rawson, 32, Alfreton, framework knitter
JAILED
John Moore, 49, Pentrich, framework knitter
Edward Moore, Pentrich, shoemaker
William Weightman, 27, Pentrich, labourer
William Hardwick, Pentrich, collier
Alexander Johnson, 24, Pentrich, labourer
Charles Swaine, South Wingfield, framework knitter

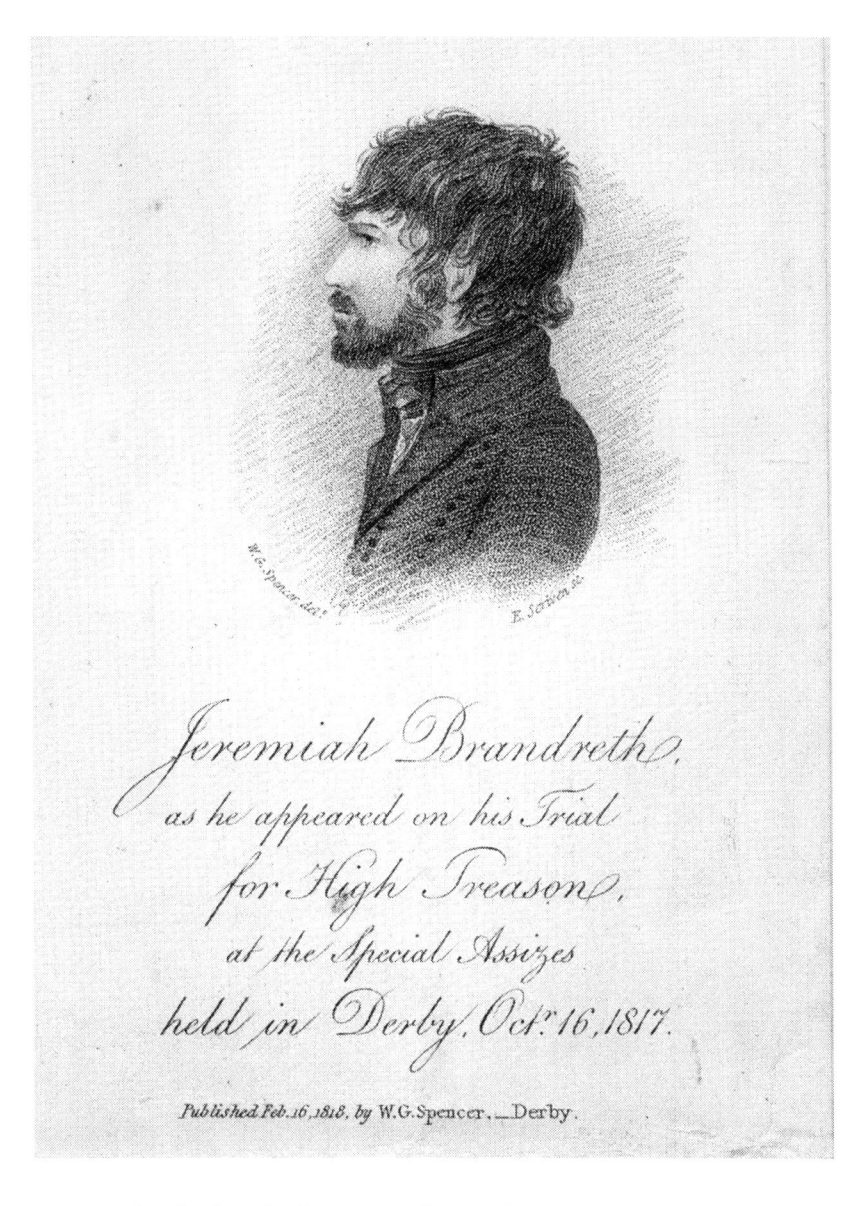

Brandreth sketched in court by William Spencer (Derby Local Studies and Family History Library, used by permission)

Farewells

After receiving the guilty verdict Brandreth accepted pen, ink and paper from Eaton the jailer and wrote to his wife, Ann[77]. He expressed his concern for her and how much he would like to see her. He was anxious that she should not travel if her advanced state of pregnancy made it dangerous. Ann replied a week later (see p53) but the authorities never passed her letter on, presumably because she condemned the *"wretch Oliver"*. William Cobbett was outraged that a personal letter should be so censored. It shows the extreme sensitivity of the Home Office to suggestions that Oliver provoked the rising.[78]

On Wednesday, October 29th, Ann arrived from Sutton-in-Ashfield and she and Jeremiah had a last meeting. Eaton allowed this to take place in his own quarters, rather than through the traditional hatch. Observers remarked upon the lack of outward emotion the couple showed at this reunion. Ann had money from public subscription in Sutton to pay her coach fare, but walked the full twenty miles, despite being eight months pregnant. She asked Jeremiah for the map he had used, but he would not reveal its whereabouts. Ann returned to Sutton the same day, having received fifty-one shillings (approximately a month's wages) from the jailer's wife Mrs Eaton to help her support her children, Elizabeth and Timothy. *The Derby Mercury* described Ann's dignified self-control:

'the external marks of sorrow were not so visible on her as they would have been in some women,' but noted that *'the affection of the heart may be the more unmitigated where the tongue is mute and the eye refuses tears.'*[79]

The execution warrant for Brandreth, Turner and Ludlam signed by

---

[77] (Neal, 1895)

[78] (Cobbett's Political Register May 16th, 1818)

[79] (Stevens, 1977) p99

Sidmouth set the date for November 7th. Weightman's name was not on it and two days after his friends were executed the Prince Regent commuted his sentence to transportation for life. The other three were also spared the quartering part of their sentences.

Ann's letter, retained by the Home Office.[80]

---

[80] (Home Office, 1817) 42/171

During his last days, Brandreth walked at exercise with Weightman and the other two condemned men, pacing firmly around the prison yard, hands in pockets, still smoking his pipe. He wrote letters to his brothers and sisters full of religious phrases. Mr Pickering, the chaplain, endeavoured to gain details of Brandreth's past; it was his failure to do so that engendered so many rumours about his origins.

Pickering was also persistently trying to find out anything he could about what Oliver might have done or said. Brandreth retained his beard and maintained silence as to his parentage and Sidmouth's spy; Ludlam and Turner were very penitent and asked Pickering for religious tracts. Brandreth's amazing detachment and calm dignity may have something to do with the fact that as a youth he had attended the execution of the radical Colonel Despard and seen his brave conduct.[81] As it was, Pickering found Brandreth frustratingly unrepentant and stoically silent about his origins until his death.

Jeremiah said he had endeavoured to make his peace with God, and he did not see why he should make any statement for the satisfaction of man. Towards the end, he was heard muttering:

'Oliver has brought me to this; but for Oliver I would not have been here.'

Government Solicitor, Lockett, was determined to suppress any mention of Oliver. Joseph Strutt wrote to his uncle, Lord Belper:

'Mr Wragg, the solicitor of the prisoners, was refused admittance to see Brandreth on Sunday last, and Lockett (not with his usual cunning) let out that he was afraid of Wragg seeing him, for that he (Brandreth) had ever since his condemnation talked of nothing else but Oliver, and that he was a murderer, etc., I hope he will speak and tell all that he knows when on the scaffold.'[82]

---

[81] (Neale, 1895) p 94

[82] (Stevenson, 2004)

The day before he died, Jeremiah wrote a last letter to Ann *'in a hand perfectly clear, plain and steady'*. [83]

> My beloved Wife,
>
> This is the morning before I suffer. I have sat down to write my last to you, hoping that my soul will shortly be at rest in Heaven, through the redeeming blood of Christ. I feel no fear in passing through the shadow of death to eternal life, so I hope you will make the promise of God, as I have, to your own soul, as we may meet in Heaven, where every sorrow will cease, and all will be joy and peace. --- My beloved, I received a letter this morning, with a pound note in it, which I leave for you in the jailor's hands, with the other things which will be sent to you, as I shall mention before I have done. This is the account of what I send to you --- one work bag, two balls of worsted, and one of cotton, and a handkerchief, an old pair of stockings and shirt, and the letter I received from my beloved Sister, with the following sum of money --- £1.12.7d. This, I suppose, will be sent in a packet to you by some means. My dearly beloved Wife, this is the last correspondence I can have with you, so you will make yourself as easy as you possibly can, and I hope God will bless you and comfort you, as he hath me: so my blessing attend you and the children, and the blessing of God be with you all now and evermore. Adieu! adieu to all for ever!
>
> Your most Affectionate Husband,
> Jeremiah Brandreth.

Jeremiah's final letter to Ann

---

[83] (Cobbett, 1818)

Retribution

On the morning of November 7th, Derby was full of people come to witness the executions. A detachment of the Inniskilling Dragoons guarded the scaffold and other detachments of mounted and foot regiments were well in evidence. The civil authorities were further reinforced by special constables and 'Javelin Men'. The chaplain gave communion to the condemned three while their fellow prisoners waited in the yard. William Turner's brother, Edward, collapsed in a fit and had to be removed. 'Manchester' Turner was in tears; Thomas Bacon kept in the background. The original irons were replaced with ones that would unlock easily, and then they were each in turn paraded around the prison yard on a hurdle – a cart without wheels. Brandreth and Turner embraced, but Ludlam was so much occupied by his prayers that he seemed not to notice them.

The three were given no time to make farewell orations, but Brandreth was heard to exclaim *'God bless you all and Lord Castlereagh'* or, perhaps more likely, *'God bless you all except Lord Castlereagh.'* The rope was then found to be tied too high for him - he was probably a man of no more than five feet six inches - and the executioner's assistant had to shin up the ladder to make readjustments.

William Turner's last words caused a stir: he ascended the scaffold with a faltering step, and on reaching the platform called out bitterly: *'this is all Oliver and the Government, the Lord have mercy on my soul.'*

Ludlam continued to mutter his repentance and then Mr Pickering led the victims in a final prayer. The Liverpool Mercury described the last moments of the Nottingham Captain:

'Brandreth appeared perfectly composed throughout the proceedings. He held a black silk handkerchief, the same which he had worn at the trial and which had just been taken from his neck

in his clasped hands while at their last devotions. This he held exactly in the same manner after life forsook his frame, He dropped quite still and seemed dead at once. His head which remained untouched, it is said, looked very frightful from underneath the white cap that was drawn off his face'[84]

After half an hour, the executioners beheaded the bodies. Brandreth's body was first to be desecrated. The executioner held the bleeding head aloft and shouted *'Behold the head of the traitor, Jeremiah Brandreth'*.

The bodies of William Turner and Isaac Ludlam were treated similarly; they were the last people ever publicly beheaded in England. They and their followers were the only 'commoners' ever to be charged with the 'aristocratic' offence of High Treason.

Thus it was that at twenty-five minutes to one on Friday, November 7th, 1817, the Derbyshire Rising was brutally concluded. The bodies were taken to St Werburgh's Church and buried in a single grave. Brandreth was laid at the bottom, with Turner and Ludlam above him. [85]

On November 9th, George Weightman learned that he had been spared the death sentence and would be transported to Australia for life. He was very ill on the voyage and nearly died, but survived and finally passed away at Kiama, New South Wales in 1865, aged sixty-eight. He was considered a worthy and upstanding citizen and received a full pardon in 1835. There is a monument in his memory inscribed:

'Pentrich Revolution, June 9th, 1817. To Mark the Life of Pentrich Rebel, George Weightman. Died Kiama 1865, [86]

---

[84] (Liverpool Mercury, 1817)

[85] (Trial and Execution of the Traitors at Derby, 1817)/.

[86] (Monument Australia, 2016)

George's wife, Rebecca lived alone working as a cleaner, to all intents and purposes a widow, until her death at the age of seventy-eight. She and their children never saw George again after he was transported. Neither Rebecca nor George ever re-married.

Thomas Bacon, John Bacon, Edward Turner, Joseph 'Manchester' Turner, Samuel Hunt, German Buxton, John Hill, George Brassington, John Mackesswick, John Onion, were transported for life. Thomas Bettison, Josiah Godber and Joseph Rawson were transported for fourteen years. Though all survived the voyage, and most lived to be freed, none ever saw family or England again. Six others received prison sentences of two years or less.

Nanny Weightman described by George Goodwin as: *'a B---h of a mother who deserves hanging worse than those condemned'*[87] lost the license for The White Horse Inn. *'The Derby Mercury'* reported:

'Ann Weightman, widow, who has kept the White Horse public house at Pentridge for several years, was convicted...of having permitted seditious meetings and, in particular, a meeting on Sunday, 8th instant"[88]

Tough old Tommy Bacon lived until 1831, passing away at the age of seventy-seven. His brother John died in 1828.[89]

Ann Brandreth reared her son and two daughters at her father's home. She re-married in 1825 to another framework knitter and had a fourth child. The Brandreth's eldest daughter, Elizabeth, died of cancer at the age of twenty-six. Jeremiah's son, Timothy, followed his father's trade as a knitter in Mansfield. The third child, Mary, was born in December, 1817. She emigrated to America with her brother

---

[87] (Stevens, 1977)p 97

[88] (Derby Mercury, 1817) June 26th, 1817

[89] (Stevens, 1977)p129

and died in 1903, aged eighty-six.[90]

Brandreth Beheaded, contemporary print. (Derby Local Studies and Family History Library, used by permission)

George Goodwin prospered at the Butterley Ironworks and remained there until his death on New Year's Day, 1848.

---

[90] (Dring, 2015)

Lord Sidmouth continued as Home Secretary, being instrumental in the passing of the infamous Six Acts, and carrying out increasingly repressive policies. He was still Home Secretary when the Peterloo Massacre took place in 1819. He died in 1844, aged eighty-five.

John Denman rose to become Lord Denman and Lord Chief Justice. He died in 1854, at the age of seventy-five.

William Oliver was whisked out of England and given a secure government position as a building inspector in South Africa. He lived the remainder of his life under the alias of William Jones, dying in 1827. His new employers who did not know his identity found him to be incompetent and suspected him of embezzlement.[91]

Henry Sampson and his large family were also helped to a new life in South Africa.

Hugh Wolstenholme the radical parson who was such a friend to the rebels was forced out of his living as curate of Pentrich in the spring of 1818. According to the *Dictionary of North Carolina Biography*, Hugh then left for America, being shipwrecked at Virginia Beach. He joined the Moravian Church and was known as 'a man of strong convictions, aggressive spirit and fearless utterances' and 'reputed to be one of the most learned men in North Carolina'.

He was involved in teaching poor children to read; one of the pupils he inspired was Andrew Johnson, 17th President of the USA, who is remembered for the Alaska Purchase and was also Vice-President to Abraham Lincoln. Hugh ended his days, circa 1875, as a celebrated hermit in a log cabin in a remote part of the Bald Mountain area of North Carolina, which would make him (if the source is to be believed) about one hundred years old. [92]

---

[91] (Cape Archives depot, GH 23/7, 1820)

[92] (Powell, 1996)

Appendix 1: The Women

Previous histories of the Pentrich Revolution have given little mention to the roles played by the Derbyshire women. The wives and mothers of the convicted rebels had to share some of the punishments inflicted upon the men. To raise funds to pay for the defence of their men-folk at trial the families sold their furniture, even, in some cases, their beds. Being deprived of the male breadwinners, the women and children were dependent upon other relatives or the Parish Relief. Most were evicted by the Duke of Devonshire's agents and some houses were pulled down. An already challenging life became much harder.

The lives of working class women in Regency times were incredibly hard. Before indoor plumbing and the modern kitchen, housework was considerably more difficult than can be imagined today and physically taxing (as anyone who has tried to wring clothes through a mangle will testify!). Raising large families in overcrowded cottages made the situation of women even worse. Between 1810 and 1820 the average number of children per family was between five and six, the highest rate ever recorded in modern British history. Married women aged between twenty and forty were as likely to be pregnant as not.

Ann "Nanny" Weightman (née Bacon) had eight children by her husband William; Isaac Ludlam and his wife Fanny (née Wheatcroft) had fourteen, seven of whom were still alive in 1817. Ann Brandreth (née Bridget) had three children in a six year marriage to Jeremiah, and Rebecca Weightman, two (possibly three) after five years of marriage to George.[93]

In addition to running the house and rearing children, working class women were expected to contribute to the family earnings.

"Almost all working-class women spent at least part of their lives

---

[93] (Mason)

earning money, principally in farm work, domestic service, factory work, or cottage industries." [94]

The women who lived on the farms around Pentrich and South Wingfield would have been involved in seasonal work on the land and every day there would be cows to milk, eggs to gather and a vegetable garden to tend.

Women *"were considered especially suited to cleaning and planting jobs: they weeded, hoed, made hay, tended flax, and planted and harvested root crops like turnips."*[95]

In stockinger families women were generally thought not strong enough to work wide-frames, but were sometimes employed using lighter narrow-frames. All members of the family would be expected to support the males by winding yarn, seaming and other tasks.

Women were not expected to hold or to venture opinions on political matters. The gentlemen radicals who were so respected by the Hampden Club members were not seeking votes for women. Henry Hunt was laughed at when he presented the first petition for women's suffrage to Parliament in 1832.

Clearly, though, women did play a part in inciting the rising. Nanny Weightman is one of a number of doughty female inn-keepers who appear in the Pentrich saga. She was an enthusiastic participant in the key meeting of June 8th, 1817, at *The White Horse*. The low opinion of George Goodwin, manager of the ironworks had of Nanny has already been noted (p64). He also remarked upon the zeal of her daughter-in-law Ellen Weightman (née Taylor) who drove husband William out to join the rebels with a poker![96]

---

[94] (Steinbach, 2013)

[95] (Steinbach, 2013)

[96] (Stevens, 1977) p97

Some local women were hostile towards the rising. Brave widow Mary Hepworth barred her doors and refused to let her men be pressed. She held her ground against an armed attack, even when her servant, Robert Walters, was fatally wounded.

Ann Brandreth's courageous walk from Sutton to Derby Goal and dignified farewell to her husband won widespread admiration.

Appendix 2: Why There? Why Then?

What caused a group of workers from a few obscure villages in Derbyshire to set off on June 9th, 1817, in a doomed attempt to overthrow the British government?

If ever there was a case of 'circumstances conspiring' this was it. The late eighteenth century saw revolutions in America and France that inspired thinkers the world over to seriously contemplate overthrowing governments that perpetuated feudal societies. The philosophy underpinning these views was published and spread by several influential writers, most notably Thomas Paine. His widely read work *'The Rights of Man'* was written in a language that allowed working people to understand his ideas. Gentlemen radicals such as Major Cartwright and Francis Burdett gave these beliefs a voice in the House of Commons and at well-attended political meetings. William Cobbett's *'Political Register'* and *'Twopenny Trash'* and Thomas Wooler's *'Black Dwarf'* were circulated widely through the Hampden Clubs which moved from being open forums for debate to becoming clandestine and focused upon action rather than words.

In Pentrich, Thomas Bacon, a self-educated and widely-read artisan with a national reputation as a political agitator, introduced local villagers to the reform movement and built up a group of followers which included William Turner who thought as he did. George Goodwin, the manager of the Butterley Ironworks labeled Bacon, a former employee, *'the great ringleader'*. In the government memorandum in what became known as 'The Green Bag Conspiracy' Bacon was named "principal promoter" and "leading speaker" of secret meetings across the north and midlands from 1816 onwards. [97]

Bacon's roots in Pentrich were obviously crucial to the revolt catching hold there. He was a relative of many of the most prominent marchers on June 9th. A quarter of those jailed at Derby in 1817 were

---
[97] (Hunt, 1819)

framework knitters as he had been, who suffered major unemployment as a result of the use of mass production techniques in the textile industry and the replacement of the quality garments they crafted, by cheap, 'shoddy' goods that could be produced by unskilled and poorly paid workers.

Some of the Pentrich and South Wingfield men had grown used to violent protest through participating in Luddite frame-breaking in response to their exploitation by the hosiers. They were used to planning, night marching, weapon gathering, intimidation and secrecy, all of which were deployed on June 9th.

The eruption of Mount Tambora caused changes to the climate that caused the terrible harvest of 1816, the worst in a decade where food shortages were frequent. Slumps in trade and resulting high unemployment worsened the situation for many poorer people across Britain. The aristocratic government of Lord Liverpool took the view that there was little, if anything, to be done and the Houses of Parliament rejected petitions from all parts of the British Isles. Popular demonstrations such as those in the Spa Fields and in Manchester were met with force. New government acts outlawed sedition and allowed indefinite detention of anyone suspected of it. Open debate was driven underground to become secret conspiracy. All the while, the debauched conduct of the Prince Regent was turning many against the royal family. The Prince received £60,000 from the Civil List in 1798, when a Stockport cotton weaver was earning about £56 a year, and economic inequality was increasing [98]

Although widespread, the disaffection lacked a national organisation and leadership. Cartwright, Burdett and Cobbett were reformers not revolutionaries and the poor transport system of the early 19th century posed logistical difficulties for meetings across the regions. For a national revolution to be organised it required someone prepared to travel widely and link the different areas.

---

[98] (Wilkes, 2015)

Such a man was The London Delegate, William Oliver, who criss crossed the north and midlands in two epic journeys, seeking to raise support for a national rebellion on June 9th, 1817. His repeated message was that thousands of Londoners stood ready to take Parliament and install a new government led by leading radicals but the north and midlands must play their part.

So the rising was invented by Oliver who did not represent anyone in London other than Home Secretary, Lord Sidmouth. The radical gentlemen he pretended to speak for and who were to form his new government knew nothing about it and would not have agreed to be involved had they done so. Without Oliver, June 9th, 1817 would have passed quietly.

It seems clear from the research undertaken by Edward Baines of *The Leeds Mercury'* that the Yorkshire radical leaders believed themselves to have been duped by Oliver; this was also the view of William Stevens from Nottingham and Thomas Bacon from Derbyshire. Many who witnessed Oliver's participation in the meetings he attended in May and June concur that he gave what turned out to be exaggerated reports of the numbers ready to take part from the areas he pretended to represent and the places that he visited. Even as late as June 7th, he was urging the Nottingham leaders to march in support of his invented thousands of Londoners and their oblivious gentlemen leaders.

To argue as White[99] does that Oliver was an inept *agent provocateur* who achieved what he did by luck and error is simplistic. This was a man who had hoodwinked sharp and watchful characters such as Pendrill and Mitchell and dozens of sceptical local leaders and who conspired with politicians and magistrates. Within a few months from 1816 to 1817, Liverpool's government had hanged seven men for frame-breaking and four for rick burning. The fact that only three were hanged in Derby for the ultimate crime of High Treason implies the government was terrified that Oliver's true role might have been

---

[99] (White, 1957)

revealed if more of the accused were to face the scaffold. The government's lawyers would not have been as accommodating as they were without a very good reason. They were obviously very worried that Oliver might be exposed on the witness stand as the originator of the national rising. Right up until the day of the executions Pickering, the Chaplain seemed as much interested in finding out how much the defendants had been aware of Oliver's doings as he was with their spiritual comfort.

At the very least there would have been embarrassing questions about how much the Home Office knew in advance of the rising and why it allowed the Derbyshire men to proceed. It would hardly have been possible to plead ignorance when the Duke of Newcastle, Lord Lieutenant of Nottinghamshire could write to Sidmouth on June 12th:

"As your Lordship is aware the plot had been hatching for some time, which we knew, and were prepared accordingly. We thought it much more desirable to let the matter come to a Crisis than to endeavour to crush it before the Designs were openly disclosed. I am very glad that we adopted this mode, as we have now not only become acquainted with what the bad People will do, but we have ascertained that the Country People are not of their way of thinking."

Henry Hunt was especially forthright and unambiguous in his summary of events:

"O! It was a horrible plot, to entrap a few distressed, poor creatures to commit some acts of violence and riot, in order that the Government might hang a few of them for high treason! ... the Government paid the freeholders of the county of Derby the disgraceful compliment of selecting that county as the scene of their diabolical operations..." [100]

---

[100] (Hunt Op Cit) p503-505

Sidmouth was exceptionally well-informed, given the relatively slow methods of communication across England at the time. His own spies and relevant magistrates who employed their own agents were corresponding with him daily during May and June, 1817. Sitting in the middle of his web of deceit and misinformation, he quietly observed events, well-aware of the disposition of the regional plotters. Even in Derbyshire, where a hundred special constables were recruited in Ripley on June 8th, the local magistrates were well aware that a rising was imminent.

But would Sidmouth go so far as to provoke a rising so that he could execute the rebels as a warning to others? In this respect, he does have some form, notably in the trial of Colonel Despard and his associates in 1803. A soldier, Thomas Windsor, is believed to have acted as *agent provocateur* in attempting to bring about a rebellion for which Colonel Despard and others were hanged and beheaded. Most of the relevant testimony came from William Francis, an alleged co-conspirator, who was seeking to avoid prosecution and whose allegations brought his own brother to the gallows. There was little other evidence, other than hearsay, and the only weapon seized was Despard's silk umbrella.

Magistrate John Gifford, in charge of arranging the executions of Despard and six others, wrote with great distaste to the Home Secretary, Lord Pelham to enquire *"When are these poor men to be murdered?"*[101] The Prime Minister who ran this show trial and employed agents was Henry Addington, soon to be Lord Sidmouth.

The final deciding element in the Pentrich and South Wingfield story was the arrival of Jeremiah Brandreth on June 5th, 1817. If Thomas Bacon had remained in charge it seems highly likely that the march would have been called off, as "Old Tommy" made his excuses a few days before and took no further part.

If Brandreth had proven to be a lack-lustre figure, even the highly

---

[101] (Conner, 2000)

politicised group assembled at *The White Horse* might not have followed him. But the dark-eyed Brandreth had the look and the presence; he had the charisma and the words to inspire loyalty; he had the intelligence, courage and conviction. An apprenticeship as a Luddite had hardened him and given him experience of violent covert action. Disappointment and poverty had left him with nothing to lose, just a bloody-minded determination to carry on, whatever the odds. He was prepared to make absurd promises of money, ale and beer to every marcher, to threaten to shoot malingerers and do whatever it took to bring his force to Nottingham.

Brandreth was a genuine revolutionary who presents as the most romantic and the most tragic player in this epic tale. The stoic dignity with which he faced his cruel death was remarked upon by all who saw it and marks him out as a genuinely heroic figure.

'J Brandreth was a man of the most undaunted courage and firmness, and possessed every talent and qualification for high enterprise.... He conducted himself very well upon his trial.' [102]

Such was the judgment of Sir Henry Fitzherbert Bt, a member of the Grand Jury which indicted Brandreth and his followers.

---

[102] (Fitzherbert, 1816)

Bibliography

(2016, March 30th). Retrieved March 31st, 2016, from Monument Australia: http://monumentaustralia.org.au/themes/government/dissent/display/96159-george-weightman

Aspinall, A. English Historical Documents 1783-1832 (1996) Psychology Press

Baines, E. (1817, June 14th). Leeds Mercury.

Baines, E. (1820). History of the Reign of King George III, King of the United Kingdom of Great Britain and Ireland. Longman.

Beckett, J. (n.d.). Nottingham; Overview: the Nineteenth Century. Retrieved March 2016, from The Nottinghamshire Heritage Gateway.

Black, E. C. (1969). British Politics in the Nineteenth Century. London: Macmillan.

Bristol Mirror. (1817, November 22).

Brougham, H. (1817). Speeches. Hansard, 1008.

Buck, A. Henry Hunt. National Portrait Gallery.

Cape Archives depot, GH 23/7. (1820). Cape Town.

Cobbett's Political Register May 16th (1818). London: William Cobbett.

Conner, C. (2000). Colonel Despard. The Life and Times of an Anglo-Irish rebel. Conshohocken: Combined Publishing.

Copley, J. S. Henry Addington, First Viscount Sidmouth. Wikimedia Commons. Creative Commons.

Cruikshank, G. Conspirators or, Delegates in Council (1817). Retrieved April 09, 2016, from Library of Congress: https://www.loc.gov/item/00652670.

Derby Mercury. (1817). Derby: Derby Record Office.

Derby Mercury. Derby. (May 6th, 1817). Derby Record Office.

Derby Mercury (November 9th,1817. Derby Record Office.

Dring, J. (2015). The Life of Jeremiah Brandreth. Pentrich and South Wingfield Revolution Group.

Fitzherbert, S. H. (1816). Sir Henry Fitzherbert Notebook Derby Records Office, D239 MF10229. D239 MF10229.

The Green Bag Plot (1819) Henry Hunt. Davison. London

Hansard, (1817). Vol 36 cc 1069-70. London.

Home Office. (1817). Home Office Papers 42/165. London: Public Record Office.

Home Office (1817). 40/9/2. London: Public Record Office.

Home Office (1817). Home Office Papers 42/166. London: Public Record Office.

Home Office (1817). Home Office Papers 42/167. London: Public Record Office.

Howell's State Trials Vol 32. (1824). London: Howell.

Howell's State Trials: The Trial of Jeremiah Brandreth. (1824). London: Longman et al.

Howell's State Trials: The Trial of William Turner. (1824). p1004. London: Longman et al.

Hunt, H. (1820-22). Memoirs of Henry Hunt Esq. London: T Dolby.

Library, D. Derby Local Studies and Family History Library, Derby.

Liverpool Mercury. (1817). P 155.

London Packet and Lloyds Evening News. London: (November 3rd, 1817).

Mason, S. (n.d.). Pentrich Revolution Genealogy. Retrieved April 01, 2016, from http://www.spanglefish.com/pentrichrevolution/index.asp

Maurin, A. Francis Burdett. Public Domain. Los Angeles County Museum of Art.

Neal, J. (1895). The Pentrich Revolution. Ripley: G C Brittain.

Parkin, M. (2014). 1817 A Recipe for Revolution.

Parkin, M. (2015). The Making of a Radical - The life and times of Thomas Bacon.

Powell, W. S. (1996). Dictionary of North Carolina Biography: Vol 6, T-Z. Chapel Hill and London: The University of North Carolina Press.

Retrieved June 6th, 2016, from Southwell and Nottingham Church History Project http://southwellchurches.nottingham.ac.uk/greasley/hmonumnt.php

Spies and Bloodites!!! No. 1(3). (1817). The Lives and Political History of Those Arch-fiends Oliver, Reynolds, & Co. Treason-hatchers, Green-bag-makers, Blood-hunters, Spies, Tempters, and Informers-general, to His Majesty's Ministers, Etc. London.

Steinbach, S. (2013). Women in England 1760-1914: A Social History. Hachette.

Stevens, J. (1977). England's Last Revolution. Moorland: Buxton.

Stevenson, G. (2004). Retrieved March 12th, 2016, from Graham Stevenson:http://www.grahamstevenson.me.uk/index.php?option=com_content&view=section&id=3&Itemid=3

The Gentleman's Magazine. (Vol 122, November, 1817). London: Sylvanus Urban.

The Parliamentary Debates from the Year 1803 to the Present Time. Volume 36. London: Hansard.

The Trials of Jeremiah Brandreth, William Turner, Isaac Ludlam, George Weightman and others. (1817). Butterworth and Sons.

Thompson, E. P. (1968). The Making of the English Working Class. Pelican.

Trial and Execution of the Traitors at Derby. (1817). The Gentleman's Magazine, 461.

Unknown. William Cobbett. Creative Commons.

White, R. J. (1957). Waterloo to Peterloo. Harmonsworth. Penguin.

Wilkes, S. (2015). Regency Spies: Secret Histories of Britain's Rebels and Revolutionaries. Barnsley: Pen and Sword History.

Wylly H. C. 1914. XVth (The King's Hussars) 1759 to 1913.

Index

Addington, Hiley 18
Ashbury, Shirley 25, 48
Bacon John 25, 35, 37, 52, 62, 63
Bacon, Miles, 35
Bacon, Thomas: 20, meeting Oliver 21, history 24, the revolution 28, 30, capture 36, jail, 38, trial 45- 47, 52, 61, transported 63, death 63, part in revolution 69, 71, 73
Baines, Edward 41-42, 71
Blanketeers 16
Brandreth, Jeremiah: execution 5-6, 62-63, early life 8-12, 15, 18, 21, 23, 23, at The White Horse Inn 25 - 27, 28 June 9th-10th 29, 31-36 betrayed by Sampson 37, put in irons 39, 41, trial and verdict 48-57, farewell to Ann 58-59, 60, 61, importance 74-75
Brandreth, Ann 8, 11-12, 28, 36, 57-58, 66, 68
Burdett, Sir Francis 14, 15, 17, 20, 27, 41, 54, 69, 70
Butterley Ironworks 24, 26, 30, 32, 34, 35, 38, 64, 69
Byng, Major General Sir John 21-21, 41-42, 44
Cartwright, Major Thomas 14, 15, 17, 20, 27, 54, 69, 70
Castlereagh, Lord Robert Stewart 41, 43, 61
Cavendish, Lord G H 15
Chief Baron, Sir Richard Richards 45, 49, 52, 53
Cobbett, William 14, 17, 48, 54, 57, 69, 70
Combination Acts 9
Cross, John 45, 47-48, 50, 54
Denman, Thomas 7, 45, 47-48, 51-52, 54, 65
Derby Mercury 6, 20, 37, 49, 57, 63
Despard Colonel Edward 8, 59, 73
Eaton, Richard, Derby Jailer 37, 57
Endsor, John 52
Enfield, Henry 28
Fitzherbert, Sir Henry 15, 74

Framework knitters 9-10, 15, 24, 55, 63, 70
Goodwin, George 24, 30, 32, 34, 38, 63, 64, 67, 68
Halton, Colonel Wingfield 27, 37
Hampden Clubs 15-16, 18-19, 24, 67
Henson, Gravener 9-10
Hepworth, Mary 29, 48, 68
Hole, Henry 34, 48
Hosiers 9-11, 70
Hunt, Henry 14, 17, 45, 54, 67, 72
Hunt, Samuel 29, 38, 52, 53, 55, 63
Hunt's Barn 27, 28
Jepson, George 32-33
Leeds Mercury 41, 46, 71
Liverpool Mercury 61
Lockett, William 37-38, 59
Luddites, Luddism 10-11, 28, 45
Ludlam, Isaac, execution 5-6, 62-63, White Horse 27, June 9th-10th 29, 32, Capture 37 Jail 39, Trial 46, 51, 53, 54, Farewells 56, 60 Father 67
Martin, Anthony 25, 48
Mitchell, Joseph 18-20, 71
Mount Tambora 15, 70
Northern Clouds 27
Oliver, William: origins, employment 18-23, 25 exposure 42-45, journeys, 45, not called as witness 47-50, 51, 52, 55, condemned by Ann 57, 59, condemned by Jeremiah 60 condemned by Turner 62, South Africa, 66, role in rising 72-73
Paine, Thomas 14, 24, 69
Pendrill, Charles 18, 20, 71
Philips, Captain Frederick, 35, 48
Pickering, Rev George 8, 59, 61, 72
Prince Regent, 14, 15, 58, 70
Rolleston, Lancelot 34-36, 48
Sampson, Henry 27, 36, 65

Shepherd, Sir Samuel 47, 48
Sidmouth, Henry Addington, Lord 14, `17, 18, 19, 21, 23, 27, 41, 43, 58, 59, 65, 71, 72, 73
Stevens, William 22, 23, 26, 33, 43, 71
Strutt, Joseph 59
Tomlinson Henry 28, 48
Towle, James 11
Turner Joseph (Manchester) 29, 52, 53, 61, 63
Turner, Thomas 34
Turner, Edward 36, 55, 63
Turner, William: execution 5-6, 62-63 White Horse 26-27, march 29 capture 37 jail 39, trial 46, 51, 54, 56, 58, piety 60
Weightman Ann (Nanny) 25, 26, 28, 63, 66, 67
Weightman, Ellen 67
Weightman, George 10, 25, 26, 28, 30, 32 capture, 33, trial 47, 48 sentence 52, 53, 56, 57, 58 grave 61
Weightman, Joseph 23, 26
Weightman, Rebecca 63, 66
Weightman, William 67
White Horse Inn 24-26, 30, 49, 64, 68, 75
Wolstenholme, Rev Hugh 21, 37, 38, 66
Wolstenholme, William 21

Printed in Poland
by Amazon Fulfillment
Poland Sp. z o.o., Wrocław